The Grandmaster's Book of Ninja Training

Dr. Masaaki Hatsumi

Translated by Chris W. P. Reynolds

CB

CONTEMPORARY BOOKS

Library of Congress Cataloging-in-Publication Data

Hatsumi, Masaaki, 1931–
　　The grandmaster's book of ninja training / Masaaki Hatsumi.
　　　　p.　　cm.
　　Includes index.
　　ISBN 0-8092-4629-5 (paper)
　　1. Hand-to-hand fighting, Oriental.　2. Ninjutsu.　3. Hatsumi,
Masaaki, 1931–　　I. Title.
U167.5.H3H358　　1987
613.7'1—dc19　　　　　　　　　　　　　　87-35221
　　　　　　　　　　　　　　　　　　　　　　　　CIP

Published by Contemporary Books
A division of NTC/Contemporary Publishing Group, Inc.
4255 West Touhy Avenue, Lincolnwood (Chicago), Illinois 60712-1975 U.S.A.
Copyright © 1988 by Masaaki Hatsumi
Printed in the United States of America
International Standard Book Number: 0-8092-4629-5
　　　02　03　04　05　BH　22　21　20　19　18　17　16　15　14　13　12　11　10　9　8　7

time with sophisticated diction, abstruse technical terms, and even words that are not to be found in any dictionary!

Major deficiencies of expression and language difficulties of non-native speakers of English who were speaking in English have been altered where possible into more natural sentences.

Occasional footnotes have been added by the translator where they might be helpful.

Japanese words (except "sensei," "ninjutsu," "ninpo," names, and words like "judo" and "kimono" that have become part of English) have been italicized, as have Sanskrit words (*"mudra"*), Chinese words (*"yin," "yang"*), stressed words, book titles, etc. The plural of the word *"dan,"* used to refer to people of *dan* grade, was a problem, since Japanese does not express the plural. Accordingly, being an English usage, "dans" was used unitalicized. The Japanese words have been retained for *shodan* and *nidan*, and thereafter, expressions such as "third *dan*" have been used.

Chris W. P. Reynolds
Tokyo, Japan

TRANSLATION NOTE

Although some of the Japanese of these intervie
was capably translated at the time it was given
Doron Navon, the entire text has been retranslat
from the original.

Unnecessary repetitions, inaudible phrases, et
have been edited out. Dr. Hatsumi's manner of spea
ing is by no means always straightforward, and litt
attempt has been made to reproduce it, since it w
felt that this would be too confusing and barely rea
able. However, efforts have been made (includi
consultation with Hatsumi Sensei himself) to clari
the many points that required it. Only a few of h
very frequently used interjected phrases (expressio
like "you see," "right?," etc.) have been retained, ju
for the sake of naturalness; and for the same reaso
some of the broken sentences and changes of dire
tion characteristic of informal speech have been r
tained, as long as the meaning is clear. This is not
say that Dr. Hatsumi speaks in simple, informal la
guage, for his sentences are peppered from time

FOREWORD

This volume is the second in a series of candid glimpses of the art and thought of my martial arts teacher, ninjutsu grandmaster Masaaki Hatsumi. The material was translated from a series of spontaneous question-and-answer sessions taped in Dr. Hatsumi's home during a succession of visits with non-Japanese friends and students. As is characteristic of Dr. Hatsumi, he often replied to the questions and comments of his visitors in this book with colorful and sometimes humorous answers that reflected his state of mind and point of view at the very moment the conversation was being taped. As is also characteristic of Masaaki Hatsumi, his point of view altered substantially with his recognition of the varying needs of the individual with whom he was conversing at any given moment.

Dr. Hatsumi remains a totally unparalleled and often enigmatic figure in the contemporary martial arts scene, a unique character composed of a wide range of sometimes seemingly contradictory components. He is the unquestioned head of nine historical martial traditions, and moves across the tatami mats of his students' training halls with all the power, authority, and centered effortlessness of one worthy of the assigned title Grandmaster. He is also an accomplished artist with brush and ink, and comments humbly that his style is unique for the simple reason that he only studied with painting teachers long enough to grasp the rudiments of mechanical technique, quitting their influence long before he unconsciously became an imitator of someone else's expression. Dr. Hatsumi is a socially oriented entertainer as well, an artist at making people feel good when in his presence, whether on stage at a large assembly or merely sharing a private conversation at his home in the darkness of the early hours before dawn. He is respected as an accomplished practitioner of the Japanese medical technique of *seikotsu*, and his expertise has always been sought out to handle emergency treatments day and night. He is also a prolific writer, combing the depths of his own experience in light of insights garnered through his exhaustive studies of the records of Japanese and world history, politics, art, and culture, to produce with amazing discipline and speed a series of technical and philosophical works that are only now beginning to emerge in the Western world through translations such as this volume.

Masaaki Hatsumi himself claims that he is an uncomplicated character, a direct and personally motivated individual merely going about the details of enjoying his life in a simple fashion as an artist. He casually attributes any of the complications that arise in his speech or writings to the influence of the spiritual ancestors who have gone before him in the martial lineages he heads. The *bujin* ("divine warrior spirit") often works its way in his life in manners that surprise even him, he admits. Therefore, he does not

in the least feel responsible for clarifying any of those personal actions and statements that confuse and confound the thought patterns of those who would force Dr. Hatsumi's martial legacy into the narrow confines of conventionality. Insist on taking his words, actions, and writings at surface level value, and you are bound to find yourself caught up in a web of conflicting mirror reflections of your own doubts and fears. Spend enough time with the man, and the contradictions melt into one another to form a clearer, deeper statement of consistent reality.

If the man himself poses a challenge for those who think they know him well, even more mystery and confusion surround his martial art. Having been awarded the title of *soke* (lineage head) for nine distinct martial *ryu* (schools or traditions) by his own teacher, the late Toshitsugu Takamatsu, Masaaki Hatsumi lives the very essence of the ninja's true philosophy in his own daily dealings with the world, his students, and his own role in life. But just what is the *true essence* of the ninja arts? Is it the wild sensationalism and eerie mystery that the novelists and movie makers would sell to audiences bored with the

lack of adventure in their own lives? Is it the pat-
terned violence and simulated manliness that a host
of self-promoted ninjutsu "masters" would sell to un-
suspecting young people who are unfortunate enough
to be lured into their makeshift academies? Is it
really being a wizard, or a black-clad mountaintop
recluse, or a lone commando-for-hire? Is the essence
of the ninja's art more than this, less than this, or
something altogether different?

This book has some glimpses at ninjutsu history's
truth, as it is manifested in the twentieth-century
world. At the same time, Dr. Hatsumi carefully, even
subtly, avoids too direct and therefore limited a defi-
nition of the ninja tradition as it was handed down to
him through the centuries and generations of Japanese history. Is there perhaps some sort of hint for the
reader there, in the very contradictions that the
grandmaster himself seems to weave around the sensitive subject of just what makes up the ninja's way of
life?

In the world of Japan in the later half of this century, the warrior arts are often regarded as an
anachronism left over from an ancient age character-
ized by radically different needs. Gone are the days
when military might, the ability to construct intri-
cately balanced alliances, and the capability to conduct effective intelligence-gathering operations con-
stituted a three-sided spear point that guaranteed
peace and security for the victor's family. In the modern advanced order of things, the Japanese conquer
through investment, and build up their personal and
national security by carefully monitoring the world
markets for opportunities to provide what others cannot or do not choose to offer. It is only natural that the
texture, make-up, and even purpose for existence of
the traditional martial arts of Japan would undergo
an extreme metamorphosis as well. Is it any wonder
that in the midst of such radical change, the peren-

nially misunderstood art of ninjutsu would allow its surface appearance to adapt to the pressures of the values and world view generated by the current age?

Enjoy the book. That is what Dr. Hatsumi would want his readers to do with it. Use it as another set of perspectives from which to further explore the value of the warrior legacies in your own life. If some of the contents spark further questions, bring new insights, or even offend, that is good. Keep questing on, keep searching, keep going. Do not expect easy answers or simple solutions here on these pages. Even I have found some things in this volume that reflect stances, opinions, and possibilities that seem to go completely against some of the things that Dr. Hatsumi has expressed to me at other times. But then that is the fun, the excitement, the joy of involvement in the warrior arts of accomplishment—ever the challenge that taunts us with the haunting questions, "Just how much can you take? Just how long can you keep on going?"

It has been many years since that night I first met Masaaki Hatsumi and asked him to accept me as a student of his art. I have grown immensely from the experience of ensuing years. It pleases me no end to see the world at large now welcoming the knowledge of ninjutsu's ages in the form of these books by the art's grandmaster. If only such books as this one had existed at the time I began my apprenticeship with the ninja! Profit well from the advantage this volume affords you now.

Stephen K. Hayes

The Grandmaster's Book of Ninja Training

INTRODUCTION

This book is a translated verbatim record of part of a series of interviews given by Dr. Masaaki Hatsumi to some of his more advanced non-Japanese students of ninpo (ninjutsu). Part of the purpose of these dialogues has been to dispel some of the misconceptions that have attached themselves to this ancient practice.

Ninjutsu, as technique, as an art, and as a philosophy, has a history that has lasted for almost a millenium. For a major portion of this time, what was taught was secret, and ninjutsu was known to very few. In feudal Japan, the ninja were a source of fear to many who struggled for military and political power, for they were trained to operate in secret and had an awesome reputation as spies and assassins. Nicknamed "kage," or "shadows," they were sometimes credited with superhuman powers, such as being able to disappear before the eyes!

It is true that the syllable "nin" of "ninja," "ninjutsu," and "ninpo" refers to "concealment" and

1

"stealing in," but it also means "endurance," "fortitude," and "forebearance."* In fact, historically, the
ninja were highly-trained men and women (the latter
sometimes called *kunoichi*) of unusual courage who
had learned to make resourceful and ingenious use of
all aspects of their surroundings, as well as of practical psychology, to enable them to accomplish their
often dangerous missions. They were certainly not
mere killers, as they are sometimes portrayed today.
Numerous unique and cleverly designed devices,
tools, and weapons that enabled the ninja to accomplish unusual feats still exist today.

The ninjas' ability to escape detection and survive
by merging into a background and by being acutely
responsive to changing circumstances is perhaps reflected in the survival of their art over ten centuries
through adaptation to the times and fulfilling the
needs of both its practitioners and of the society in
which it lived—and still lives. For there have always
been those who have valued alertness and awareness
over the following of rules and the accumulation of
memorized "facts," have treasured sensitivity over
form and formality, have prized living for the moment over spending a lifetime dying.

And the times are indeed a-changing. This once
secret and shadowly art has now achieved consider-
able popularity, and unfortunately, through misun-
derstanding and exploitation, a certain amount of
notoriety, in many countries of the world. But the
living knowledge of the ninja is now freely available
for anyone interested enough to look beneath the surface. The principal source of this fascinating teaching is Dr. Masaaki Hatsumi, the *Soké*, or grandmaster, of no less than nine ancient schools.

The current world of martial arts is ailing. Modern

* *Ja* = person; *jutsu* = art, technique; *po* = principle, way,
doctrine.

"martial arts" have become firmly attached to considerations of strong and weak, and of competition. But in this fixation, the real spirit of *budo* cannot be found. Tigers and other wild animals are indeed strong fighters, at least from the viewpoint of violence, and yet these strong fighers have fallen victim to man, a comparatively weak creature. Why? Men, from the earliest times, realizing their own weakness against these powerful beasts, devised means of capturing and killing them. And what this meant for man was not merely a victory in some competition: it was what enabled mankind to survive. I have given these interviews in order to bring back some reality, meaning, and credibility to the martial arts, for what in general passes for martial arts today is a collection of rule-bound practices mainly intended as vehicles for competition. I am not trying to disparage them as *sports*, but from the point of view of true *budo*, which has to be concerned with real conflict, they are very limited indeed.

The reasons why I choose Doron Navon, Jack Hoban, and Charles Daniel for the interviews in this book are these: they have correctly and sincerely pursued the true essence of *budo*, not only through ninjutsu, but also through other martial arts of Japan and of other countries. Also, for them, this pursuit takes precedence over the economic considerations that can become attached to *budo*—indeed, it is deeply rooted in their nature, and they are all fine representatives of the Bujinkan Ninjutsu dojo.

The way to learn, to become a martial artist of excellence, is not to go about judging a partner as strong or weak, good or poor, and not to pay any attention to rank and such trivialities, but simply to look and to perceive the characteristics of the other person, and to keep going in one's own practice. This is what leads to the real victory—this, and also the kindness and openness of heart to help others to discover and overcome their faults. These will eventually enable a person to maintain superiority in a real conflict.

In teaching my students, there are periods when I constantly emphasize the importance of *flow*, of *fluidity*, in *budo*. This flow is the equivalent to the flow of blood in our veins, the flow of life. This flow continues even when the ninja is standing still. It links each move, each technique to the next. My method of teaching is designed so that techniques cannot become fixed in the mind, as part of some carefully kept store of knowledge, for once this happens, the techniques lose their life, their life comes to a stop. In a real fight, survival is the important thing: for the martial artist, life must not come to a stop. The flow must go on; he must walk on; he must keep going. . . .

During my recent visit to London to give a ninjutsu seminar there, one of the students remarked that my techniques are always new and original. I replied that he was right, for I will not be teaching again what I taught in London. My techniques always arise from the moment, are always different and fresh. This freshness is energy, life force. This is one of the most important things to understand in martial arts. So I always stay away from old techniques. And, as a device to prevent students from getting any fixed idea of how a particular technique should be, I avoid giving them time to memorize any technique. In this way, I'm trying to instill in them the essential *flow* from which an utterly unlimited range of fresh movements and new techniques springs forth, like miracles from a magic fountain.

The ultimate purpose of real martial arts is to maintain peace and freedom. Martial arts are for maintaining happiness, and to bring others the experience of happiness. It is to foster this kind of martial art and this kind of spirit that the Bujinkan Dojo exists.

Dr. Masaaki Hatsumi

Background of Doron Navon, 8th Dan

Doron Navon, from Israel, is the only non-Japanese who has the 8th dan in Togakure-ryu Ninpo, and is a *shihan* (senior teacher) of the Japanese Honbu (the center and fountainhead) of ninpo—all of the other *shihan* being Japanese. He speaks fluent Japanese and English, as well as Hebrew, and acts as an interpreter for Dr. Hatsumi in Japan and abroad.

He went to Japan at the end of 1966, and stayed eight years, mainly studying ninjutsu and judo. In 1974, after acquiring teaching certificates in both arts, he returned to Israel and opened the first ninjustu school outside Japan. This school is now the center of Israeli ninjutsu. Besides his 8th dan in ninjutsu, he has a 4th dan in judo from the Kodokan and is a teacher of the Feldenkrais method, which works on improving the quality of movement through the coordination and integration of the motor and nervous systems and the thinking processes.

Doron now travels around the world teaching the philosophy and technique of ninjutsu and the unique method of Feldenkrais. He continues his studies of ninpo with Dr. Hatsumi, often returning to Japan to improve his skill and understanding of the art.

Background of Jack Hoban, 6th Dan

A former U.S. Marine captain, Jack Hoban trained in ninjutsu under Stephen K. Hayes before going to Japan to further his knowledge under the direction of grandmaster Masaaki Hatsumi. Although he teaches occasional seminars and runs his own *taijutsu* club in the New Jersey-New York area where he lives, he considers himself a practitioner rather than a teacher. Nevertheless, he holds a *shidoshi* license from the grandmaster and is authorized to teach the art of ninjutsu.

Jack Hoban has written two books on the arts of *tantojutsu* and *bojutsu*, and is now working on a third book on his training philosophy and how it applies to various levels of contemporary life in the United States. He holds a master's degree in business administration and is an executive of a major financial services corporation.

Background of Charles Daniels, 5th Dan

Charles Daniels has studied the major martial arts of Europe and Asia, settling on ninjutsu as his life's guiding art. He has written several books on ninjutsu. He tours the U.S. and Europe, giving seminars on the art of the shadow warrior.

The Translator

Born in Africa almost half a century ago, in what is now Zimbabwe, Chris Reynolds has spent most of his life involved with languages (ancient and modern), medical matters (Western and Oriental), Indian philosophy, and martial arts (boxing, judo, aikido, and ninjutsu). He speaks a few of these languages—some quite badly—and works mainly as a freelance medical translator, at which he thinks he is somewhat less unskilled. He has lived in Japan for 14 years, and is married, with two young children. He now studies ninpo under Dr. Hatsumi, for whom he acts as an occasional interpreter. Given the choice, he would like to be younger, less clumsy, more intelligent, and able to fly.

PRELUDE

Hatsumi Sensei (H): Those of you who have come to Japan from the USA probably have got quite a different impression during this seminar of martial arts as practiced here, as compared with what you have so far been used to in your own countries. So I'd like you please just to say what you want about your experiences.

Ed Sones (ES): In the States—I come from Texas—it seems that most of the training, including my own training for the past few years, has been too intense and has been using too many techniques—trying to learn technique after technique—and you come over to Japan and you realize the depth of the *feeling* of ninjutsu. It's something that you can't explain, and you just have to experience. And *this* is the place to do it.

Bill Atkins: I agree with the criticism of tension and of trying to use one part of your body more than another part, instead of everything being together. Here I learn a lot more about everything moving at once, moving as a single being toward whatever I want, not overreacting to something that's happening but just flowing with it. And the people I've met are some of the most beautiful people that I've ever encountered.

Anthony Netzler: I'm from New Zealand, and I feel the same. I enjoy developing the mind as well as the body. And the aspect of everyone being friends, like a really close community, rather than everyone trying to compete against each other.

John Samlon: I'm from Florida. My feeling is almost the same as everybody else's. I find a deep respect and love for all the people I meet here. The students and instructors are almost like a family, and the training has been completely different than what I've learned in the States. I find that I'm more relaxed. I'm more able to use the body and the mind. Before, I was sort of blank-minded.

Mark Hodel (MH): I've come from America to Japan to experience Sensei's *budo* and to learn to fight without feeling as if I'm fighting.

Guus Lekanne dit Deprez: I came here from Holland especially because this is the art where you don't have to use muscle power and speed. Everything depends on body, distance, and timing, so even if you're not so strong, not so tall, and so on, you can still use it. Other martial arts, if you're small, you can't use at all against large people. And the different ways of thinking: if the situation is changing, you change with it, you're not stuck on one thing—that's how I like to think. And you get a great feeling for how to do it. Maybe you can do it after a fashion, but you get the *feeling* from Sensei.

Demetrios Papanicolaou: I come from Greece. My past experience in other *budo* arts gave me quite another attitude to learning how to fight. We would build up muscles and fighting spirit by hard training; there were no friends, no love, but it was necessary to develop hate between competitors in contests.

Ninjutsu, I believe, is a really warm art with love. It comes from soul and heart. You learn to grow into this, and you learn you don't need power or muscular strength. But you use your mind and something from space, something more and deeper than is in all the other martial arts. If somebody can feel that, if a person can understand, it's wonderful. So it's the love that brings me here, and I'm going to continue to come every year, because I want to get that feeling and sensitivity from Hatsumi Sensei more and more while I am with him. He's the only one I want to learn ninjutsu from.

Gadi Lissak: I'm from Israel. I train in ninjutsu mainly because I enjoy the training, and that's the way I was taught in Israel, and that's also why I came here—to enjoy it. Thank you.

Larry Speakman: I'm from America. I came to Japan to learn the way of the warrior, and to integrate myself into the world and integrate my body and my mind. With Hatsumi Sensei and with ninjutsu I think I've done that.

H: Thank you.

What I am really hoping for, as various people come here from overseas, is that they will gradually, one by one, come to understand what I am teaching, and that each one in turn will finally grow into a fine instructor of this art, not like most of those teachers who have preceded them. I want them to become instructors who understand freedom.

The *taijutsu*[1] that I teach is founded in freedom, and the feeling that we are looking for arises out of freedom of movement. This freedom is so important. A person who does not appreciate how precious freedom is cannot understand my *taijutsu*.

---

1 Literally, "body art," this term is variously translatable as "way of moving," "manner of using the body in executing techniques," "physical behavior," and "coordination," and tends to imply flowing and coordinated management of the body in movement.

Each person must take individual responsibility for his actions and behavior, so that these spring from a feeling of freedom and are free. Those who do not have a correct appreciation of freedom are going to create trouble for those around them. To a person who cannot grasp the true idea of freedom, freedom looks like selfishness. But what is to be valued is the type of individualism that is born from and lives in freedom. And this idea is reflected in the statement, "Above the heavens, below the heavens, only I exist, unique and absolute,"[2] which I believe did originate from the Buddha.

Anyway, if you have anything to ask about the martial arts, please go ahead and do so now, and I will answer. Don't hesitate. Ask freely—whatever you like—and I will reply freely and openly.

ES: What would you say would be the thing that would most determine the greatness of a warrior?

H: Well, for me, though I've studied with many people, I would just look to Takamatsu Sensei as my model of greatness in this respect. And there is only one thing that I would single out, and that is to *keep going*. This attitude of *keeping going* has lasted for a thousand years. This is what I do, and it's what I want everybody to do: to *keep going*—to persevere in the right way, in the true way. And what is this truth, this true way? It is the truth that has kept ninjutsu alive for a thousand years.

MH: Why did you decide, Sensei, to share your *budo* with other countries and people outside Japan?

H: It is simply because people in this world need to love each other. So that *budo* is something to be

---

2 Spoken, according to Buddhist mythology, by Prince Shakyamuni in his cradle. For those unfamiliar with Indian philosophy, the word "I" here may perhaps be understood as referring to the "I" of the enlightened person, which the enlightened person knows is universal and the same in all of us. (In Japanese, *"Tenjou tenge yuiga dokuson."*)

shared with everyone living on this earth, as a matter of course, and of natural, good behavior. In the same way, you know how, when you share food with others and they all savor and enjoy it, it can taste better for you, too. . . .

Well, now, first of all, before I start to discuss what Doron has to ask. . . . We have here Nagato, ninth *dan*, Ishizuka, ninth *dan*, and on this side, Oguri, ninth *dan*, Kan, eighth *dan*, Doron, eighth *dan*, and finally Jack, sixth *dan*.

Anyway, the Bujinkan has had its turns and twists of fortune, but now I have finally succeeded in a real sense to the rank of *Iemoto*, the head of this school of *budo*, under the name "Toratsugu."[3] So, what I'd like to do now is talk about our future direction in the *Bujinkan*, in answer to any questions you might have on it. I would also ask you to speak about any feelings or opinions of your own about this. And so, Doron, would you begin with your questions, please. . . .

---

3 The name means "Heir of the Tiger" or "Tiger Successor."

I

Doron Navon (D): People in Western countries attach a lot of importance to a person's grade, especially in relation to the *dan* grades, and I wonder if you'd give us your opinion on this. And also, related to that, how do your ideas on grades differ from the usual ways in which they are regarded in the other martial arts?

H: Well, I've been involved in martial arts for about 50 years now, and over this period I've observed the attitudes that people have about the *kyu* and the *dan*. For example, someone will come into my *dojo*[4], and it has often happened, someone who has done another martial art—judo or karate or something—and there is a good feeling about this person and in his attitude. And sometimes, you know, people from arts other than mine have a really beautiful feeling to them. I'll sometimes feel, even after quite a short time, as I watch this person practice and see what he has

---

4 Training hall.

brought with him from his previous training, that he is well worth a *dan* grade in this art. But I'm well aware that when people come from other countries and are awarded a *dan* grade after only a short time, they feel it's pretty strange.

In my own case, I now consider that I have at last become a true *Iemoto*, but I believe that I received the formal recognition from my teacher, Takamatsu Sensei, very prematurely—in the same way as, in the old days, full mastership in a martial art might be conferred on a samurai even before he had attained the requisite skill. A young samurai would find a *budo* master who would train him in a wide variety of techniques for a period of only a few days. The master would then dismiss him, saying something like, "Well, I've initiated you into the finest points of my art, and you now have all that you need from me. You are now a practitioner." The young man would then go from place to place and put what he had learned into practice in contests and so on, until he had really grasped the "feel" and "sense" of the art deeply as part of himself. Thus, it was up to him to nurture and polish his own proficiency and understanding.

But the system of ranking people according to the skill that they have already developed is something that's tied up with sports. It's like the line that has to be crossed, for example, or the tape that must be broken, for an athlete to be acknowledged as winner, but such things do not exist when it comes to actual fighting. And the way I regard grading is free of this idea of a fixed mark.

So if you take other *budo* like, say, karate—now, karate has its own *taijutsu*. It's not as if *taijutsu* is part of ninjutsu alone. My teacher often used to say that even a shopkeeper has his *taijutsu*—the way he bows, rubs his hands, greets his customers, and so on. And of course, dancers have their characteristic movements, their *taijutsu*, too, so I call our *taijutsu* "ninpo *taijutsu*," in order to distinguish it from shopkeeper's *taijutsu*—and, for that matter, from night-club stripper's *taijutsu*! And I base my *dan* gradings on the criteria of ninpo *taijutsu*.

But it's when there is a misjudgment that a big problem can occur. I expect that there will be a question about that later, though, so I'll leave it for now. But one can judge a person's proficiency in *taijutsu* from the way he or she acts when holding something. It needn't be a weapon. One can even assess a grade from what happens when somebody takes a *deshi*,[5] or when somebody changes his or her way of life in some way. It just shows so clearly from the way a person acts. So if you give an undesirable person a stick, sooner or later he or she may well start hitting someone with it. A person's character shows itself even through a weapon. So not only *taijutsu*, but also *bojutsu*,[6] for instance, can be used to judge a person's proficiency in *taijutsu*. In very early times, they used to use wooden staffs (including the six-foot *bo*[7]) for fighting—these being the equivalent of swords in the days before bronze and iron weapons existed. Later, such staffs were used when swords were unavailable.

Other kinds of weapons used by the ninja were those for throwing, and a person's handling of these is equally revealing of his or her ability in *taijutsu*. For example, there were the *shuriken*,[8] and, also, one would attach weights to a cord so as to make them fly a long way through the air for use as weapons (like the *fundo* of *fundojutsu*[9]), and so on. There were even esoteric techniques of "throwing one's will": achiev-

---

5 A pupil, student, or disciple.
6 A Japanese martial art using a staff as a weapon.
7 The staff used for *bojutsu*.
8 Generally star-shaped metal plates about 3″ in diameter with sharpened edges. These were thrown somewhat like a frisbee and were capable of making a very nasty, deep wound.
9 *Fundo* is a metal weight such as may be attached to each end of a chain (or cord) for use as a weapon, employing the techniques of *fundojutsu*.

ing an effect on an opponent at a distance through willpower and psychic force, for example, by the use of *kiai*.[10]

So I feel that the most correct way to assess a person's grade is to base one's judgment on all of these three skills: unarmed *taijutsu*, the use of hand-held weapons, and the use of weapons for throwing.

You see, this has a parallel in Japan even in relation to governing the country. There are three sacred symbols of sovereign rule. Firstly, there's the mirror. This is related to, or we can use it to represent, *taijutsu*, and you find that in many other activities, for example, in Dalcroze eurhythmics and in dancing as well as in ninpo *taijutsu*, you may sometimes use a mirror to correct your posture or movement reflected there. Then, the next thing is the sword, which in the old days, only the high-class people—the samurai, the teachers—were allowed to have. And thirdly, there is the *magatama*, a beautiful ornamental bead shaped like a cashew nut, which is polished and is used as the symbol of the spirit, of the heart. These three emblems have been symbols of government in this country ever since ancient times.

In *budo*, too, there are three important essentials: first, seeing and knowing oneself, one's own strengths and limitations; second, the sword of discrimination, of decisiveness, for eliminating faults, weaknesses, and the unnecessary; and last, the sincerity, feeling, devotion, insight, and understanding of the heart. These are for me equally the essentials for sensing, for knowing, a person's grade as for organizing and

---

10 A kind of shout used for achieving a high degree of psychic concentration in a moment. It may be used to cause momentary shock in an adversary or to have a resuscitating effect on a person who is in some way incapacitated. *Kiai*, translatable as "concentration of energy," "harmony of the spirit," or simply "breathing together," also refers to the finely tuned timing that is essential in the martial arts. The word can also be used for a flash of genius or insight.

leading the *Bujinkan*. This is my approach. This too is a matter of "keeping going."

D: Please, would you speak about how ninjutsu has developed in the modern world?

H: Well, of course, there were stages. Right at the beginning, when I succeeded to the Grandmastership of ninjutsu, the ninja didn't have the type of black clothes that they wear now, and they used a *montsuki* (formal kimono) with a *hakama* (split skirt), so that they looked a bit overdressed. But they even used to climb trees and so on in this getup! Next, that man who was doing some study on sumo, Mr. Andy Adams, arrived and was the first foreigner to come and see my ninjutsu; and after that, during the Korean War and then the Vietnam War—as you might expect—a number of Americans and others came one after the other to find out about ninjutsu. And that was when the ninjutsu boom, or "ninja boom," started.

The reason for this boom and the attraction to ninjutsu itself, even for the Japanese, was that people expected extraordinary or fantastic feats. It was natural, really, and it was the mass media that were to blame for putting out these strange ideas about ninjutsu. They didn't come to us first and find out what it was really about. I'm quite convinced that this was the problem. They kept saying things like, that people could use it to make themselves disappear, that ninjutsu was an evil practice, that it was for assassination. All the time they were running down ninjutsu, continually trying to spread the idea that it was a shameful thing.

But anyway, attracted by the sensational side of these articles, people naturally started trying out ninjutsu techniques, and injuries resulted—and of course they went and criticized ninjutsu for it. According to what I've heard, this was happening a lot in the U.S. when the ninjutsu boom got going there.

In this way, the mass media publicized quite a

mistaken notion of ninjutsu, but this gave me the opportunity of writing about the true ninjutsu, and I find it very gratifying that I have been presented with this chance. Now, I've also made some videos to show that ninjutsu is not some group of dirty or magic tricks but a well-founded system. As I have always said, it is something that well-balanced, sensible people may practice.

Now we are in the midst of the second ninjutsu boom in my lifetime, and this has spread all over the world, but in fact, the real ninjutsu boom—what will be the third stage—is still to come. I think that we will have another boom, this time of the true ninjutsu.

In America, Stephen Hayes has now come to understand about this, and Jack Hoban too understands. Now that Stephen is seventh *dan* and Jack is sixth, we're beginning to see some really fine instructors over there. And in Europe there are some excellent instructors, and then there's you, too, Doron (now at eighth *dan*). So now the time has come, I believe, when a true and correct understanding of ninjutsu can spread throughout the world. This is very important. And now I think that these unnecessary accidents and incidents will stop.

D: What does ninjutsu have to offer those who love martial arts?

H: Well, as I've already said, a lot of people who have studied the martial arts have come to learn from me. Through long experience I have learned how to give them what they need. The most important thing for them, you see, is to let go of and lose the forms and styles of movement that they have learned in the past, so as to begin to absorb the feeling, the *sensibility*, that I am trying to convey. After all, there are all these various styles and techniques that people have learned—all kinds of things like kung fu and karate, judo and aikido—you know, all the various fighting styles, differing from country to country.

What I'm trying to get people to do is drop their habits—the various physical habits that they have developed in practicing these styles, so that they can give all their attention to *feeling*, to *sensitivity*, and to *good* feeling. The combination of this feeling with the feeling of my art, the ability to unify the two—*that* is the important thing for such people to progress in ninpo. In each of the martial arts there are characteristic forms and practices that can transmit the right attitude and sense associated with that art, and what I want people to do is dissociate themselves from these habitual forms while coming to understand the *sensibility* that is part and parcel of ninpo; and in this way I am trying to transmit my art.

D: Can you give any *practical* ways in which the way of thinking, or the way of looking at the world in ninpo, can help in a person's daily life?

H: Well, what one can do is. . . . Firstly, a person can learn self-control, to bring a good balance into his or her life. This is the first, the essential thing. Of course, there are people who have never learned this control and balance properly. For example, just as in the case of Christ and Judas, however wonderful a teacher may be, there's always someone among his pupils who cannot understand properly, who becomes disaffected and breaks away. So it's not a matter of just teaching everything and then expecting people to conduct themselves properly.

I don't want to judge people merely on the basis of their having studied under me. It all depends on the quality and feeling of the person. I think this is very important. But it's the ability to live a *balanced* life that I'm saying is the most important thing—the ability to conduct all aspects of one's life in a self-controlled manner—*this* is what I am looking for. I don't try to force it at all: people are free.

Now, in some ways, this word "free" has a frightening aspect. A tiger, for example, is free, as in the old story in which a tigress knocks her cubs into a deep ravine and will rear only the ones that can make their way back to her on their own. That's freedom, too, right?—for both mother and cubs. And both recognize it—it's mutual.

There's freedom from the responsibility for one who can't stand on his own feet, on the part of the mother; freedom of choice for the cubs as to whether they make enough effort to find their way back, or give up; the freedom for the successful cubs that comes from learning what the mother teaches. It's the same for me, too. I recognize my students' freedom, and they acknowledge mine. This again is balance; this is control. And this is what I believe has made possible the continuous history of ninjutsu that has lasted a thousand years. As a result, undesirable people gradually drop away and disappear of their own accord. As their learning acts as a mirror, they begin to see the unsavory aspects of themselves and are shocked or embarrassed into leaving the school.

It's funny that in my ninjutsu, a person might learn how to disappear, but if he starts using such knowledge for some evil purpose, he disappears of his own accord! So one should avoid avarice, dependence, and presumption on others' kindness. Avarice and also dependency which puts a burden on people are both deplorable and *must* be avoided; and the avoidance of both of these is an essential element of training and of discipline. So it's quite predictable that a person who has some inflated ambition, like a greed for fame or a desire to be better than anyone else in the world, will simply disappear. At the same time, it's an amazing thing. To do things simply, plainly, and without fuss is one of the most important qualities. The simple life, right?

I'll tell you what my teacher once said. You know, Takamatsu Sensei had the most amazing skill. His ninpo was so strong that people used to say he was as fearsome and ferocious as an old tiger![11] Well, anyway, when he came back to Japan after the war he went into business in Yamato. An old friend who came to see him there apparently once told him, "Well, Takamatsu, they used to call you the old tiger, but now you seem to have become just like a pussycat!" Takamatsu Sensei laughed and replied, "Well, at least a cat can be pretty sure of staying alive!" That was the kind of balance and stability he had. It was a matter of life: as a "tiger" in those days he might have been killed, but a cat is an animal that can be cuddled by any little girl or might be petted and looked after by anyone. This ability to switch between power and gentleness and still retain one's stability, this balance, this control—it's really vital, I think.

D: When I trained with you many years ago, there were no foreigners and very few Japanese training. Training was very hard and very dangerous. Today, your training is very soft, very relaxed, and very playful. What's the reason for this change?

H: I suppose it's a matter of achieving a certain degree of skill. There's an old proverb, "No fights for the wealthy," meaning that people who have plenty of money don't get into fights. And by the same token, when one attains mastery of many martial arts, it's no longer necessary, I think, to go hard at it anymore. You see, I've been practicing martial arts for fifty years now, and indeed there were periods when hard training was needed. At the present moment, though, the reason why such hard training is not required is that the Bujinkan has expanded a great deal, and a lot of people are training, so we could have a lot of injuries happening if people went at it hammer-and-tongs as we used to, right? People would get hurt. So, in order to allow many people to learn without injuring themselves, and to enable those who already have

---

11 Sometimes rendered as "Mongolian tiger."

some understanding of what I'm teaching to make
plenty of progress without being held back by injuries—that's why the training has changed like this.
Gradually, I think I myself have come to a certain
level of maturity, too.

D: In the Western world, people tend to look at a
person's physique—his muscles, his size—as a criterion of his power and ability. But in ninjutsu, I've
seen that exactly the opposite of this criterion seems
to apply; the less strong a person looks, the better he
is. Can you explain this?

H: Well, you remember I told you Takamatsu Sensei's remark about being a tiger and getting killed,
becoming a cat and living? This is just the same. At
the same time—well, you know, this man does karate,
this fellow does judo, this guy's a wrestler, and if you
look carefully you can tell—anyone can—what fighting style each will use. And then—it's all over!—at
least if you're a true martial artist. For a true martial
artist, to see an opponent's strength is to know what
kind of attacks he is likely to use; such a person would
never reveal himself in this way to an opponent, and
if he's really skillful he will win lightly, without
much effort, in a real fight. For example, if the opponent attacks from the front—well, in a sport the two
have to compete face-to-face—but when a conflict is
in earnest, there's no reason why one should not attack from behind, and such attacks are common.
From a sporting point of view, though, this would be
judged a cowardly foul. That's the long and the short
of it, simply speaking. So, where the enmity is real, a
person may be attacked on the toilet, or during love-
making, or at mealtime. It's when people are feeling
secure and at ease in wartime that they are most
often wiped out. But when a *man* goes to the toilet, he
takes his pistol in his hand, so he should be OK,
right?! *(Laughter)*

In sports, people often speak of favorite techniques,

don't they? In judo, for example, they talk about how great somebody's favorite technique is, or they ask, "Hey, what's your favorite technique?" "Oh, mine's *osotogari*," and so on. But this kind of thing can be very dangerous in real life, as opposed to sport. You tell someone your favorite move and, being fore-warned, he'll do his best not to be caught by it. Some-times, people will ask a real martial artist, "Sensei, what's your favorite technique?" But when they come to me with that question, I reply, "So you want to try and kill me, huh?" One should never ask another person's favorite technique—it should be regarded as an absolute taboo—just as one should never show one's own. Nothing at all should be shown. In fact, it is better to seem to have no experience at all in martial arts. Hmm. OK?

D: Yes, thank you. When you speak to us you usu-ally emphasize the spiritual and artistic parts of the human being. Why are these so important for a per-son who practices martial arts?

H: Well, for one thing, it's a matter of balance. If you know only one aspect, you lose the ability to see and know yourself; if a person practices only the techniques of his (or her) martial art, as he improves and becomes more skillful, he builds up an inflated illusion of his own ability and of himself. People lose sight of their own, and their martial art's, shortcom-ings. This is a terrible state to be in. It's really impor-tant to be always aware of and in touch with one's own faults. This is why I am practicing other arts and doing other activities. The link between them all is in the feeling, the inner attitude.

The composer Mendelssohn once said, "Where con-versation ends, music begins."[12] Again, the common thread is in the *feeling*. So, after *taijutsu*, what comes

---

12 Translated from a Japanese version. I have been unable to find the original quotation (presumably in German).

next? It's the sword. And after the sword? Heart and
mind. And it is by building the links between all
these aspects of one's life, by keeping constantly in
touch with the current that flows through them all,
that one becomes connected to a greater life—a life
that one could call infinite or eternal. This is why I
have students do many different things—it's to discover the next stage.

D: During the first years of the period that I
trained with you, Takamatsu Sensei was still alive,
and I remember your telling us that, one day during
training, he fell on his knee. It was after his eightieth
birthday. You mentioned that it was something
which had never happened before, but it had now
happened after eighty years. And you said that it was
a sign that his end was close. My question is, how,
really, can a person train to such an old age and still
be in such good health? In most of the martial arts,
there are so many injuries collected during the years
that the person is limited when he gets a little bit
older. Do you have anything to say about the daily life
and the way of thinking that can help in connection
with this?

H: Let me tell you first a little bit about Takamatsu
Sensei. When I first met him, the first thing he used
to do when he got up in the morning was give himself
a friction rub with cold water. And then, he always
used to exercise the twenty dogs—they were spitzes—
that he kept. He used to take them for walks every
day. He would eat a lot of tofu. In fact, he used to have
a very balanced but a very varied diet, eating food
appropriate to his years, taking exercise suitable for
his age. But he wasn't like other people of his age. He
used to walk fast enough to leave us behind, and this
was something he did every day. But, you know, we
go walking now every day; after a few drinks also, we
go for a walk. But people usually go to sleep after
drinking, and this is no good for the health. So when-

ever I have been drinking, I go for one- or two-hour-long walks, and then, for food, I eat unpolished rice.

But, to get back to Takamatsu Sensei. He had low blood pressure, so he used to drink *Yomeishu*[13] on getting up, and he would follow that with a cup of salt water—this was to strengthen his nerves. And so, in those days at least, the way to live a long time and stay young was to live a life of *ten'i muho*, that is, a pure, harmonious, and natural life. This concept of *ten'i muho* implies freedom, but in spite of that, if the key to that freedom is not understood, the freedom itself is entirely lost. I think you'll gradually come to understand that.

D: And then, what about the way of exercising and of practicing?

H: As far as practices were concerned, to put it simply, when Takamatsu Sensei led a practice, there was not even one occasion when he got us to do any warming-up exercise. It was just a sudden, "Come here. . . . Do this . . .," and so on. When we used real swords, it was the same. So I would always do preparatory exercises. It is vital every day to do some movement and loosening-up exercises—and it's also really essential to do some "loosening-up" exercises that will work at the mental and feeling levels as well. Physical exercises alone are not good enough. More subtle work, too, is absolutely essential for maintaining the balance between the more subtle aspects of the human being and the physical. Just physical practice is no good at all. Is that OK?

D: What about the way of thinking and the daily life and practice that can help—in relation to growing old?

H: Yes, mm. You see, even people who don't practice *budo* also do such exercises—everybody does, for

---

13 A general tonic drink popular in Japan that contains some Chinese medicinal herbs.

their health. It's not just the *budoka*. Many people sleep without clothes on—like Marilyn Monroe! Many older people in Japan throw cold water over themselves every morning and live to be over eighty, still brimming with health! I'm not trying to tell you to copy them, you know—just because I wake up in the middle of the night and go for walks doesn't mean that I want you all to do the same thing. Just that, in emergency situations, it's sometimes necessary to move around at night. Not that I want this to sound like some kind of self-glorification, but I train so that I'll be able to change according to the situation whenever it is required.

When I went to San Francisco a little while ago, although I had only two hours of sleep a day for two weeks, I was able to complete satisfactorily all the things I had to do over there! I gave people a lot of training and didn't let them sleep much, so of course I wasn't sleeping, either. I got an average of only about two hours a day for 14 days. All the same, when I returned I found that I wasn't tired. This was just ordinary training. It was thanks to my—by ordinary standards—irregular and unhealthy way of living that I was able to do this. It's true that this sort of activity can be labelled irregular and unhealthy, but in fact I've been able by everyday training to live a way of life that transcends the negative effects of things. For example, as I've said, after I've been drinking, I always go for a walk for an hour or two, whereas most people just go to sleep after drinking. Of course, it has to do with the force of will, or spiritual strength. But this is all part of the same continuum of strength and weakness that everyone is on.

D: In the last training, you said that the stronger a fighter becomes, the more love he should have. Could you explain this, please?

H: Oh, that's easy, surely? Look at Nagato here, or Ishizuka. Look at Kan, too. To a child, the father always looks strong, right? But the father loves him, hmm? It's the same in *budo*. That's all it is. It's quite simple—nothing special. All *my* love goes on women, though! *(Laughter)* Got no children, that's why! But these women nowadays—they're a bit too strong, you know! It's safer *not* to love 'em, really! *(Laughs)* You can put that in the book, too!

D: Nowadays, when so many people who have read a little about ninjutsu and trained for a few months immediately go off and write a book about it and start teaching, it is very difficult for the ordinary person to know who is genuine and who is not. Do you have any advice about this: from whom can the beginner learn? And I'd like to ask about your videos, too, in this connection.

H: Well, you know, I don't think it's such a bad thing that people should put out books on ninjutsu—everyone's got to live, right? It's just that, while they still have an immature understanding of the subject, it would be better if these books were not published, because they tend to stay around for so long. I've always said this: as soon as a person who writes such a book gains a little more understanding and skill, he often regrets writing it. "What a fool I was to write such stuff when I knew so little!" At the same time, it's very difficult to express ninjutsu in writing.

A video is better than a book for this. It's probably better for learning to have both a video and a book. That's why, after writing a few books, I've now made some videos, and I'm intending to make them available all over the world. And I think these will help people understand what ninjutsu really is, as practiced here. So it's fine that books have been written, and that people should go on writing them—it enables them to make some money, which they'll need if they're going to get to Japan and stay a while here. It's just that, if they put out something embarrassingly bad, they are judged on the quality of it, even later. It can be quite unfortunate, quite unpleasant.

D: So are you suggesting that if someone sees the

video and sees the true movements of ninjutsu, he may recognize that you are a real teacher?

H: Mm, you see, there are eighth and ninth *dan* instructors studying under me, but none of them have written any books. And, as you know, I have told you all not to take any notes while you are practicing. Even if you did, it would be of no use: if you write something down, you'll actually lose the sense of what I'm trying to teach. But there are periods when you really want to write, I know. At those times, I don't mind. But, you know, when I wrote things at such times, it was just a waste. This is the reason why I have said that what really needs to be learned is the *feeling*, the aspect that has no form or shape. In *budo*, the most vital aspect is that which does not have a form and cannot be expressed. It's also something that cannot be seen by the opponent—which gives you the chance of doing what you like with him. So I knew when I started writing books that, whatever I *wanted* to say, it would be possible to express only the most minor and least significant aspects of ninjutsu. For that which is infinite is inexpressible. I want my students first to understand this deeply and only then to try to put words to ninpo, whether in books or in speaking about it.

D: Do you have any recommendations for the person who is starting training in ninjutsu?

H: First, to watch my videos and read my books. And at the same time as that, to study with a real instructor—a teacher who has come and studied in Japan and who is capable of transmitting, of *infusing*, the feeling and spirit of my art. One must absolutely not go to any *budo* instructor who cannot convey this feeling. Just watching the videos and reading the books, though, is of no use: it's impossible to pick up the feeling. It's the same with anything. There are three elements—a bit like the three emblems or symbols that I spoke of before. Nothing can be done without this third element—it can't be transmitted by books or videos. It has to come through the instructor, which means, in the U.S., through Jack, sixth *dan*; in Israel, through Doron, eighth *dan*. That's why I want people to learn from proper instructors.

Also, it is very important that the instructors be open and honest about their grades. I don't want anybody puffing himself up or trying to teach beyond his capability. Let people who are *shodan* acknowledge it and those who are *nidan* recognize that, and teach their students as such. None of these third dans posing as tenth dans—it's bound to lead to a fiasco. This is essential, hmm?

D: From you I have learned that in ninjutsu, to develop only the physical part is really not enough. But still, *taijutsu* is basic to ninpo. Could you explain why, and could you say how *taijutsu* can help in the development of aspects beyond the physical level?

H: It's not so much a question of aspects beyond the physical, but rather, the thing is to bring the *taijutsu* and the mental and spiritual side of a person into harmony, like *yin* and *yang*. With this, one can switch between power and gentleness, between positive and negative. This may be a little difficult to comprehend, I'm afraid.

So what is *taijutsu*, then? Obviously, it's a matter of moving physically, but at the beginning one moves because the mind—the conscious mind—tells the body to move in a certain way. Sooner or later, the subconscious takes over this function, and the person moves more instinctively. But of course it's no good if the movements of *taijutsu* become mere conditioned reflexes. So there's that difference. And there's a balance between subconscious *taijutsu* and conscious *taijutsu*, but it is the subconscious *taijutsu* that is the more important.

In the structure of human consciousness, if we

were to represent the subconscious by a value of 9, then the conscious awareness would have a value of 1; and when a person reaches fifth *dan*, he then begins to enter the world of the subconscious. From *shodan* to fourth *dan*, a person is working with conscious awareness, rather than the subconscious, over those four steps. But then, if we represent the conscious by 4 rather than 1, then the subconscious must be represented by 4 times 9. That's 36—thirty-six stages in the subconscious! So there is the old Chinese proverb, "Instead of thinking of thirty-six different ways of fighting, the best course is just to run away" (discretion is the better part of valor), which I believe is a response to a subconscious instinct. That is what the expert ninja really does. Do you understand that?

D: In the early 1970s I alone was allowed to watch you carrying out the test for the fifth *dan*, for a person to become a *shihan*, or top instructor. You said at that time—and you still repeat it today—that a person becomes a real teacher only after he has reached the fifth *dan* level. Could you say more about that?

H: Well, of course, this is just as I was saying a moment ago. In the field of *budo*, it is *nothingness* that is the most important thing. After all, if you show nothing, pretend nothing, think nothing, *are* nothing, there is no way for you to be caught by the opponent's attack. Moreover, you can move without letting the opponent know what you are going to do. We call that "emptiness." Emptiness exists, but it does not make its presence known—the opponent is not given any hint. In the martial arts, this is the most important thing for staying alive. That's what being fifth *dan* means. To escape from a blow from behind—it's something that animals can do, right?—without having years of practice. So passing the fifth *dan* test involves a kind of loss, a dropping of something that is essentially human but which impairs our sensitivity and separates us from our own subconscious. But nobody must imagine that by passing the fifth *dan* test he has become some kind of magician or something. Then he would *really* be in trouble!

D: You are a master of nine schools of martial arts, a mastership that has been passed on to you by Takamatsu Sensei. The histories of those styles go back hundreds of years to ancient China, India, and Japan. This represents a vast amount and breadth of knowledge and wisdom. Could you please elaborate on this?

H: Well, as for the amount and the breadth—it's really quite a simple thing. After all, if a man lives in nature, then to the—we might call them the commands of nature—he. . . . You see, Takamatsu Sensei used to speak of gods as "inexplicable mysteries," and these inexplicable mysteries can manifest themselves in reality when one practices these nine arts. And at some level of awareness, there is a kind of communication—I don't know how—with some presence in the universe; and it is at the behest of some being that I, for example, am alive. I feel this kind of thing again and again. Although I am of course one single person, in some way I am not just one person. I have a body, but I am not just this body and so on, but I can feel an assimilation taking place of my spirit or my psyche into the great Existence itself. Or should I perhaps say an *absorption* into it, an entry into the divine world. This feeling comes to me from time to time. And this is not some weird religious hallucination, you know!

D: I have known you now for twenty years. But still, each time I come to you, you keep teaching me new things! How do you do it?!

H: This is just as I keep saying: there's no point in getting caught up in one's thinking or in one's store of knowledge. The most important point, the absolutely vital key to this, is what my teacher called "the heart of God and the eye of God." I suppose that what you ask is something to do with a mastery of this key. I think it springs from the understanding of the *Kihon Happo*[14] of my *budo* and of the three symbols, again; and this is why Takamatsu Sensei used to say that the practice of *taijutsu* could bring about miraculous happenings.

---

14 The basic forms of ninpo *taijutsu*.

Doron Navon, 8th *dan*

It is sometimes preferable, when disarming an attacker with a knife, to be in no hurry to remove the weapon. Instead, the defender should first entrap the attacker's arm by the judicious positioning of his own arms, and then take the knife. Doron is one of my finest students, with a excellent mastery of the subtleties of *taijutsu*.

In *budo*, the movement of the feet is vital. So also is suppleness, just as in Doron's Feldenkrais work. Also, the whole way one walks.

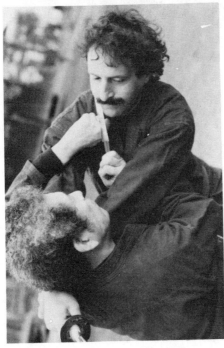

Watch out, Doron! It's not just your two hands: the way to "cook" your assailant is to stop him from moving his feet—no need to try to break the balance of his whole body.

There's no point in trying to grab with the hands alone. Doron has trapped the attacker's arms, and his left foot is positioned to neutralize any movement of either of his attacker's feet—the control coming from the movement of the *whole* body.

Here's another variation! The legs are the most important, *then* the hands. Using the feet to pivot, Doron got both body and legs moving and turned the table on his opponent, getting him all screwed up! See? You don't need any strength at all!

Don't just use the sword to cut: the legs and feet—and the body with them—have got to move so that if the opponent shifts he gets cut.

Doron has a quiet and gentle nature. He is a very perceptive and sensitive man, who has calmy, smilingly, and correctly absorbed the feeling and subtleties of this art.

Holding the opponent's sword with your own, make whatever adjustments are necessary to control it and gain the edge over him. Remember the principle of the lever, too.

In avoiding and dodging, don't move too far: *just enough* is just enough. You get it, hm? But it's not your *head* that needs to understand!

My teacher, Takamatsu Sensei, demonstrating the *takeori* ("bamboo-breaking") form of the *gyakudori* method of holding. A flexible bamboo is difficult to break; but the ability to move, sensing instantly the point where an adversary's suppleness is most limited, is the mark of a master.

Takamatsu Sensei and the author (taken in the former's house).

A talk with Takamatsu Sensei
could go on for a thousand
years without being exhausted
of interest. I used to be like an
eager child, sitting in his home
fascinated as I listened to him talk. He spoke with
everything—body, mind, heart, and spirit—and his words
touched each of these in me, like sparks of light and
understanding.
The talking role falls to me now, as I pass on what I can
to my students—my martial arts friends.

A blinding technique in hand-to-hand combat (demonstrated by my wife). In Japan, too, the eyes are said to be the windows to the soul, and an attack on the eyes can reach deeper than is at first apparent.

Ukigiri ("floating out"). In response to the enemy's sweeping attack the defender springs up lightly ("floats" up), cutting as he returns to earth; making maximum use of the freedom of space.

Niramiuchi ("glaring hit"). Their stares locked, the two adversaries nullify each other's attacks. (Doron Navon has the sword.)

II

Jack Hoban (J): What is natural food for a Japanese is not natural food for a foreigner. Do you think that the diet should be different for each country?

H: I think it's obvious that dietary habits differ from country to country. But one thing that is important is to know what a great effect diet has on a person's character and on health. Food and health, food and character. It's often said that if children eat a lot of junk food, it tends to make them rough and violent. And if they eat only meat, for example, they can become very wild, almost like animals. That may not always be so, of course. But it seems that if they drink milk, as well as eat a lot of meat, some degree of balance may be achieved, so that their behavior is more controlled, especially if they also have plenty of vegetables, and so on.

As far as my own eating habits are concerned— well, at first, I was not very healthy and was too fat, so the doctor told me to lose weight. I went on a diet of

unpolished rice, and vegetarian food including tofu
and *natto*.[1] I'm embarrassed to admit it, but I was
really so fat, and I used to eat anything; I had a waist
of about 44 inches and weighed over 200 pounds! I
started getting ill. I'd really been foolish about my
body, overestimating its capacities. But then I
realized how much harm I was doing to it. After that,
I started eating raw vegetables at the beginning of a
meal, then unpolished rice, and finally, some low-
calorie food. In three months on this diet, my waist
returned to about 35 inches. Anyway, with this rice
and tofu, vegetables and so on, I had no salt, sugar, or
other seasonings or flavorings. By avoiding such
things, one can keep one's body free of most harmful
substances, and one becomes sensitive to other toxic
chemical food additives. If you always eat palate-
pleasing food with a lot of seasoning, you lose your
sensitivity to these things.

In the old days, I often used to visit Takamatsu
Sensei's home, and his wife would always serve tea.
Each time she did so, she would say where it came
from: "This tea is one grown in Uji," or "This is the
tea of Shizuoka," in her old-fashioned way. On some
days, she would make tea fifteen or twenty times, and
every time it would be a different kind. I really used
to enjoy it, drinking her teas. One day, all of a sudden,
Takamatsu Sensei challenged me, "Do you know
what kind of tea this is?" I was quite taken aback by
this. "If it were poison, what would you do?" he went
on. Indeed, you can't protect yourself against every
poisonous substance by tasting it and remembering
the taste. It's a matter of the sensitivity of your taste
buds, a matter of perception. And as you develop this
sensitivity, you get to realize what should not be
eaten or drunk.

So, one lives in order to do this. Things that smell

---

1 Fermented soybeans.

Jack Hoban, 6th *dan*

Singer and guitarist, former Marine captain Jack Hoban seems to pick up the feeling that I try to teach through his musical sensitivity.

strong are avoided as much as possible. The ninja practices an "odor-free" discipline: he avoids garlic, leeks, all spicy foods, salty things, oily things, and so on. If his body gives off the smell of something he has eaten, for example, when in hiding, his adversary may become aware of him. On the other hand, if he does not eat such foods, he becomes far more sensitive to external stimuli. As my teacher used to tell us, when in the mountains, the ninja is usually nowhere near women, and he eats only mild foods. As a result, my teacher said, the ninja becomes so sensitive that he can become aware of a woman who might come into his general vicinity, even without actually seeing her, and he can also tell her age and even her occupation.

And fasting also is probably a useful part of the ninja's discipline, for the same kind of reasons. I had an experience of a really strict fast when I was ill, and for about eighteen months I had only a pot of yogurt every day—as some of you know. That was really amazing for me. I wasn't even in a fasting center. I feel that it was a kind of divine gift for me. Or rather, it was the *illness* for which I feel so grateful to the Almighty.

J: Japanese people are structured differently than Westerners. Does that mean that natural *taijutsu* would look different for a Westerner than for a Japanese person?

H: Well, you know, in Japan people often say that Westerners are weak in the hip area. Our ways of life are quite different, right? Because Westerners use chairs, whereas the Japanese sit down on the floor, their hips are weak, according to Japanese people— martial arts people, judo people, everyone. It's become a cliché here. But it's quite untrue: people from the West have very strong hips.

Their area of weakness is actually the knees. For anyone with long legs, the knees are bound to be a bit weak. The hips are strong. So when Japanese want to strengthen their own hips, it's their knees that they work on. What Westerners need to concentrate on is their way of walking, to improve that. I told you just before, when we were standing up, didn't I? You're standing with your knees locked; you should try keeping them a little bent. And every day, when you walk, you should keep your knees bent and take only small steps. It's not so much for health that you need that, but for your training. Also, when I am sitting, like this—hmm?—I sit with my legs folded. The adductor muscles, which bring the knees together, are kept stretched, you see? This is good for strengthening kicks and for loosening up the hip joints.

And then, Doron, you see, you sit with your back hollow. Is this from your Feldenkrais work? No? Well, I don't know why, but anyway, I suppose you sit like that naturally. Takamatsu Sensei used to sit like that. When he got tired he would always stretch his spine backwards. Then he would sit like this for a while, and then stretch back again, and he could go on like that for long periods of time. When people fall into depression, they tend to slump, like this, right? But when they're enjoying themselves, they open up their chests like this, perhaps with mouths open in laughter, too, hmm? Of course, in order to maintain one's balance, probably in some disorders of the autonomic nervous system, it's important—as well as pleasurable—to extend the spine from time to time. You should constantly watch things like this.

And then, there's the big toe, which is related to the liver and spleen through the (acupuncture) meridians. These two organs seem to be the most strongly affected by the action of the nerves. The liver is the organ with the strongest capacity for regeneration—and this is one of its great strengths, I think. But I believe that strengths should be further reinforced, and to do this you can hold each big toe and revolve it round and round, or if you don't like moving it round, you can sit cross-legged and move the feet and the big toes. Stretch the back, too

Takamatsu Sensei said that the legs—actually from the *hara*[2] down—must never be allowed to get

---

2 Belly.

cold. He even gave me a woolen *haramaki*[3] once for this, while I was ill. And he told us always to move the toes, keep them moving, even when lying down. But don't get confused and do it with the middle leg—it gets plenty of exercise when you're lying down! *(Laughter)*

J: You said in your book, *Hiden no Togakure-ryu Ninpo*—and I am paraphrasing this—that an evil person will naturally give a victory to a person with a clear heart. Could you elaborate on that?

H: Well, the most important thing to remember here is that the person who does dishonest or evil things is not properly aware that what he does is bad. This is one point. Now a person of good will has the ability to repress undesirable behavior. This is *nin*,[4] the *nin* of ninjutsu. This idea exists, of course, in religion, too, and in Zen: *ninniku seishin*.[5] There is a saying, "Enduring insults and humiliation, I drop all rancor, I desire no revenge," which implies bearing no hatred and holding no grudges. Christ taught the same, when He said, "Love your enemies." This is tremendously important in our lives—indeed, I think it is the foundation: the power to show forbearance, the strength to restrain oneself. This is essential in training.

For example, people come to a martial arts *dojo* and may undergo some pain in practice, right? They are in the role of receiving attacks more and more, and then, as their *taijutsu* improves, their training comes to involve dealing with attacks at a psychological level, too. A person who can endure this patiently and with perseverance without losing his equilib-

---

3 A band of cloth wrapped around the abdomen, worn generally by older Japanese men, to prevent chilling of this area.
4 Restraint, endurance.
5 The spirit, or attitude, of forbearance and fortitude.

rium will achieve a great deal. (That's why a ninja's clothes are sometimes known as "the armor of forbearance.") And the temperament of a ninja may be observed in this way. The uniform is like the *kesa*[6] of the Buddhist priest, and Takamatsu Sensei used to call it "a taste of Zen."

J: The mass media image of the ninja includes constant reference to *mudra*,[7] *jumon*.[8] Did the ninja really have their own finger-entwining system that was separate from that of *Mikkyo*,[9] which you can read about in any book on the subject? And do you teach it? Why or why not? When in the training would anybody be taught this kind of thing? Also, can a non-Japanese person who does not really understand Eastern religions find any real value in *kuji*,[10] in your opinion? Is *kuji* also included in the teaching of *taijutsu*? And are the *mudra* required—I mean, do we have to practice the *mudra* to get a high level of *kuji* feeling? I know that's a tough question, but. . . .

H: There was a time when I myself went through a lot of doubt and questioning about the *kuji*. Now, in Japanese Buddhism, the figure 9 was the highest of all, in gambling too, the strongest. The combinations *kuppin* (9 and 1) and *shippin* (4 and 1), however, were stronger. If 9 and 1 are added, you get 10, of course, and this sum was then considered the highest number of all. There was also a saying related to this, "Even after a 9, never a 10," which had several inter-

---

6 A brief surplice worn by Buddhist priests.
7 *Mudra* (Sanskrit, meaning seal, symbol): one of many codified symbolic gestures or postures, especially of the hands, sometimes said to have psychic effects.
8 Chant, incantation, curse, the chanting of a *kuji* (see note 10).
9 Esoteric Buddhism.
10 Literal meaning: "nine Chinese characters." A short phrase said to have the power of a spell over an opponent when spoken or intoned by a full-fledged ninja.

pretations, including ideas like, "Don't go too far,"
"Do not teach the most extreme methods," and "Even
in victory, do not kill or maim an opponent." As for
shippin, the sum was 5, and 5 was said to be the
highest number in the Age of the Gods in Japan—the
highest in a religious sense—according to tradition.
But I probably haven't made that very clear to you.
Takamatsu Sensei said that this whole thing about
the 9 and the 10 was related to Buddhism, but he also
insisted that both religion and martial arts are seek-
ing and working toward the same goal and that the 9
and the 10 are in this sense the same. I believe, too,
that the ultimate aim of *Mikkyo* and of Christianity is
one and the same. Do you understand? It's a bit
difficult. . . .

D: Yes, yes, that's fine, Sensei. Thank you. So could
you please go on to the second part of Jack's question
about the *kuji*? Do you teach it? And why do you do so
or not do so?

H: Oh, yes, I teach it, I teach it. But rather than
memorizing the *kuji*, it's better to perfect your
taijutsu. You see, if you tried to learn the *kuji*
"*Gakorai tosha akuma fudo*," which, if it's intoned
properly, can stop an opponent from moving, or
"*Fudo mugo*," which can bring about a loss of sensa-
tion in an opponent, it would be absolutely useless,
until you had perfected your *taijutsu*.

And so, as I said before, my teacher used to say that
when a person is really accomplished in *taijutsu*, as-
tonishing things begin to happen. Every one of you
here knows this. For example, in the U.S., when Stephen Hayes tried to hit me on the head from behind—
well, you're meant to intone the *kuji*, right?—but
even without my saying it, he couldn't hit me, could
he? And so I told him that *that* was what *kuji* meant.
Of course, inexplicable things like this happen in
religion, too, for example, in Buddhist training; and

without thinking, or perhaps even knowing, about things like the *kuji*, many eminent Buddhist priests have done such things. And Christ, of course, performed many kinds of miracles, as you know.

D: So when does one begin to learn the *kuji*?

H: When your *taijutsu* is perfected, I will teach you then. When a person's *taijutsu* has reached a level of development suitable for the *kuji*, I will teach him. If I did not wait, the results could be disastrous. If I taught it too early, the student would probably just get hurt. Anyway, people who aren't good enough don't particularly want to learn it. Also, it's got to be taught correctly. The instructor has to teach it correctly, as I would. When the student is at the right stage, is of sufficient caliber, I will teach him the *kuji*. It would be extremely dangerous to teach somebody who is not suitably prepared: it could result in his death. To put it simply, if in a critical situation he tried chanting the *kuji* thinking that he would disappear, and then didn't disappear, for example. . . . Well, you understand?

D: Yes, I see. And would you teach it to foreigners as well as Japanese?

H: Oh, yes, I'll teach anyone whose *taijutsu* is good enough. But there is still nobody who has reached that level. Even in Japan, there are very few such people. And that's why I haven't taught anybody yet. In fact, it's just as if it doesn't matter whether the *kuji* exists or not.

D: But you know, Sensei, there are people teaching it all over the place!

H: Yes, but the simple fact is that there is not a single person who knows how to. It's simply a fraudulent affair. Teaching an unqualified person and then telling him, "Oh, you can do the *kuji* now," is just a fraud. Only somebody who has the capacity can do it. Just the same as the fifth *dan* test—which is not something you can teach—the *kuji* can't really be taught, and until a person has mastered *taijutsu*, there's no point in trying to use it.

D: And then there was Jack's question about whether the teaching of *taijutsu* includes *kuji*.

H: Yes, there's *kuji* in *taijutsu*, *kuji* in *kenjutsu*, in *bojutsu*, in ninjutsu. . . .

J: Then, are the *mudra* required to develop a high level of *kuji* feeling?

D: What is *mudra*?

J: *Mudra* is—ah—the hand position where you entwine your fingers.

D: Ah, yes. So, Sensei, he asked whether the *mudra* is necessary for producing the feeling of *kuji*.

H: Oh—as in *Mikkyo*? No, there's no need for it. No, you do that after your *taijutsu* is properly developed.

You see, the 9 and the 10—*kuji* and the *juji*[11]—the attainment and mastery that they represent, are born out of keeping going, out of long perseverance. Nobody knows when it may happen. It varies greatly from person to person. For example, in my *taijutsu*, as you know, there are so many aspects that you can't learn, that you can't teach; even if you are taught these things, you can't do them, and even if you try to learn them, you can't do them. It's just the same with the *kuji*: it's impossible to learn, it's impossible to teach. It's just like *taijutsu*.

So as far as my *taijutsu* is concerned—well, all of you have become very skilled now, but the fact is, it's beyond skill: for further growth and understanding, it's no longer a question of skill or of lack of it. I suppose it's to some extent a matter of age. . . . But, just as I often say, there are plenty of painters, but only one Picasso. But who is going to be my Chagall? Who will be my Matisse? I am waiting to see.

J: Next question. It is obvious that the Grandmaster and his students live very normal and unpreten-

---

11 Literally: "ten Chinese characters" (as opposed to *kuji*).

tious lives. Why do you now seem to seek high-level contacts? And what do you mean by "white-collar martial art"?

H: In the past, as I've often said, the system of transmission of a teaching from a master to a single pupil has been pretty rigidly followed. It was felt to be desirable that each school of *budo* should be represented by a single person, by the leader of that school's tradition. I think that the number of people who studied in these schools varied according to the period. But those who had come close to the top in terms of their sense and feeling of the art that they were practicing were in fact the medium, the fertile ground through which the tradition was transmitted. The kind of people who had that sense were naturally spiritually very fine human beings. If they had not been, they would not have been able to approach so close.

For that reason, if I am going to teach anyway, I feel that to teach people who show promise and seem to have a future in the society in which they live, people of worth, people I have referred to before as "white-collar" people—to make people of *this* sort the medium of my art is likely to contribute more to the world, to be of more value to other human beings. So I think that this is the best way for me to proceed with my work. To try to teach undesirable people would be very dangerous: what they learn might be misused, and so on.

It's a bit like the problems surrounding the peaceful use of atomic power. After all, people who have their own livelihoods get on with their own lives and don't go in for robbery and violence and the rest. And it's important from the viewpoint of the teacher, too, as a human being, that his pupils should be people of stable and secure character, people who live productive, not destructive, lives in the world. And that is the direction I want my teaching to go.

J: Our training is very gentle and relaxed now, but

a real fight has a lot of emotion to it. Now, without starting a fight or sparring, how does one prepare himself for the emotional aspects of a real encounter by just doing *taijutsu*?

H: A real fight is something that cannot be re-created, especially if some deadly weapon is used. Therefore, it's absolutely vital to find a way that will enable one to win and to get into a winning frame of mind. If you can't do that, you will lose. And also, if you are going to really fight somebody, it is essential to know your own ability. For this reason grades are needed. If the opponent looks stronger and more skilled, you make yourself scarce, right? You know when to leave, hmm? That in itself, in my opinion, requires some training. Even if you're weaker, there's a way for the weaker man to win. One formula of *budo* is this: display your weakness to be strong. Or to put it the other way round, if you don't know this formula then, however strong you are, you can be easily beaten by somebody weaker in a real encounter.

D: Sensei, would you say a little more about "displaying your weakness"?

H: "Displaying your weakness" means—if you generally appear weak, you don't usually get people coming to fight you. But then, if you are attacked and you have been displaying your weakness, the attacker is unlikely to be prepared for any retaliation. He comes in to hit you, and without any effort on your part he is in range for you. Then you have the chance of winning quite easily, and this sort of thing really happens. So it's quite different from a sport, because if the fight is in earnest and you feel that you're weaker, you'll stay away from danger, from where the opponent is strong. But if you happen to find yourself in danger, then you use whatever means you can—*taijutsu*, whatever, depending on the situation.

For example, if you think you are weaker, you

might use a pistol. If a person is unaware of this simple formula, and he starts thinking, "Well, I've been studying ninjutsu, and I'm pretty good now," he might easily get killed—I might get killed myself, if I did that. Let me make it quite clear: *this* is what *budo* is—recognizing your own capabilities *and* your own weaknesses, however strong you may be. Some people do know this, though, even if they have had no experience of *budo* training. A man may well be killed by a woman—after all, pistols are available in many countries.

Please think about this carefully: it's important. However strong a man is—he might even be a world boxing champion—in this day and age, someone just has to pull a trigger, and he's dead. If a person doesn't think about such simple things and doesn't attach any importance to them, when it comes to the real thing, he could lose his life at the twitch of a finger, whatever *dan* he might have. It's necessary to remember this. So nobody should imagine that martial arts are somehow almighty. A man must realize that he is alone in the world, and he needs to know his level of ability as far as fighting and conflict are concerned.

Many, many martial arts people don't understand this—they're brainwashed by their teachers to think that their own *budo* is the strongest. And there are even schools where the students—even the teachers— are quite happy to be brainwashed in this way! This is a terrible thing to happen. Being brainwashed is just like being blind, and so I have absolutely no desire to do it to anybody. What I always want is for you to purify your *heart* (heartwashing!), and that's why I give you this.

D: This?

H: *"Shikin haramitsu daikomyo."*[12] OK.

---

12 This phrase is used as a prayer or salutation at the start of a ninjutsu training session.

J: You seem to consider ninjutsu training to be rather straight-line *taijutsu* training only. How do you feel about people adding other things—other practices and teachings—to the training? Do you care about it? What do you think about it?

H: I feel that, in the circumstances in which those people work, and with the values that they have, it's fine.

If their ability in ninjutsu is so limited, it can't be helped. It is important that they should do what they can to help their students understand, and so as to do that, they may make use of these other things. But of course, *taijutsu* must be made the basis—the main ingredient. If it isn't, what is taught becomes like an overdiluted cocktail where the alcohol no longer has any effect, or like food without any flavor. It's all too easy to go wrong in teaching ninjutsu.

J: Can you tell us a little bit about the other students who studied with Takamatsu Sensei? For example, could you tell us some more about Mr. Akimoto?

H: Indeed, I think that Akimoto Sensei was a true disciple of Takamatsu Sensei. He was a gentleman who observed the traditions carefully, and he really understood his own system of values well. For example—you see, he was my senior in *budo*, and when the title of *Iemoto* was handed down to me by our teacher, although I was far younger than Akimoto Sensei, he was really happy for me. I was still at that time not really much of anything, and from Takamatsu Sensei's point of view, Akimoto Sensei had many far more developed skills than I did. For example, at the Tone River once, he was wearing a sword, and a skylark suddenly came flying past. In a flash, his sword was out, and the dead bird fell to the ground. That shows the level of skill he had. I have heard many tales of his martial exploits, and I know a lot of stories of his encounters with prominent *budo* men whom he defeated.

But the really important thing to realize in *budo* is that technique alone is worthless if the man loses his equilibrium, his inner balance. If a man does not have some other major strength, it does not matter how far he develops his technical skill—he will be beaten in the end. So I reckon that Takamatsu Sensei probably felt that a person needs to be born with some other major talent whereby such a situation can be prevented.

There were many others senior to me who were also more skilled than I was, but I suppose now that I was the guy who, in my teacher's view, could preserve this tradition that had already been handed down for over nine hundred years and who could keep it alive satisfactorily one way or another. Then, Takamatsu Sensei died, and for fifteen years I have been thinking, "Oh, things are not satisfactory. . . . I've got to do better. . . . This won't do. . . ." And now, I've just awakened, now that I've been to America and back as Grandmaster of this school, to the fact that things *are* OK, and progress *is* being made. As Grandmaster, I've now introduced myself as Toratsugu, the name that Takamatsu Sensei allowed me to use. And then, as if in reply to all this, I was elected to the *Black Belt* Magazine's Hall of Fame as Instructor of the Year. To me this was as if Takamatsu Sensei were saying to me, "It's OK, young feller. You *can* call yourself the *Iemoto* . . . that's fine now!"

The timing of the news of the *Black Belt* award, which came just as I decided to assume the title of *Iemoto*, was like Sensei remarking, "Yes, all right, that's fine. Call yourself Grandmaster, too, if you want to, son! You've done pretty well so far—I can see that . . . !" This is what occurred to me at the time. And quite apart from any happiness I felt, I thought of what a great gift this was for everyone in my *budo*, and I hoped that I would be able to pass on the teaching correctly to everyone. I even hoped that I would in this way be able to repay my debt to my own teacher.

J: Your ranking system seems to be based on how much the person understands the feeling of your training, particularly for foreigners. Yet the rank certificates say "ninpo *taijutsu*." Are you worried that some people will teach bad *taijutsu*?

H: No, I haven't been worried about that sort of thing at all. There'll be books coming out on it, as I have said. But, you know, with a person of ill will, his true nature shows itself in the way he moves. It's really an amazing thing how he shows his true colors in his *taijutsu*. But as I've often said, the true sense of each person's grade is confirmed by everyone's positive response and recognition of the grade. It is so much better for everyone to recognize it than for me just to decide in isolation. Here's a good example: the fifth *dan* test is done in front of the other students, right? And the candidate carries the good wishes of all the others with him. I feel that it's really important that a student should carry the blessings of the others to his new grade and feel their support and joy when he gets it.

From now on, when instructors are teaching in other countries—instructors who have not come to Japan—it should generally take about three years to reach *shodan*. This is important. Instead, though, if someone comes to me in Japan and has some kind of understanding of the feeling of my art, I'll promote him more quickly. This is because we will need instructors soon, all over the world. But I hope that some of these people, on returning to their own countries, will come to realize that they can't go far on their own. For example, they will see that the feeling alone is not enough, and when this happens, those who are really serious and genuine about it and are aware of their shortcomings can go to Jack's place or to Doron's to learn. The time has come now for this. The timing is good, and I'm very happy about it. But the ones who do not recognize their own inabilities will simply lose their own pupils, sooner or later, when something goes wrong. OK?

J: This is the last question. It's a long one. In history, businessmen and warriors are always portrayed as being of separate philosophies and motives. Do you agree? Can there be such a thing as a warrior-businessman? And should his training be different in any way from regular *taijutsu*? If you want to attract white-collar people to the art, they will have to see the value of ninpo in terms of their professions. Do you agree?

H: Well, of course, the two have a number of points in common. In the long history of ninjutsu, businessmen had a role to play, just as martial artists did. But in the society of the Edo Era,[13] although it was called a samurai society, the samurai largely tended to turn into businessmen. The peaceful times of the end of the Edo Era were fairly protracted, and in this period of peace, samurai for perhaps the first time became able to make a living by teaching the various *budo*. This commercialization was a sad thing. At the beginning, they knew little about business, just after the Civil Wars Era.[14] They had to live, and so they learned business. There was no choice. And so it was necessity that forged the *bugei*, the martial arts at that time. As the peace and stability stretched on, people appeared who were forced to make their livelihood from the business of teaching *budo*, for their fighting skills were no longer in demand. As far as I am concerned, as long as the *budo* were correctly preserved, it doesn't matter by what route they have

13 The Edo, or Tokugawa, Era lasted from 1603 to 1867.
14 The Civil Wars Era (*Sengoku Jidai*), which gave the samurai plenty of fighting to do, had ended not long before the Edo Era.

come down to us. Just as long as the core, the essence of the teaching, has been preserved, it is fine. This is all.

There are people in every era who, however adverse the environment, are not corrupted, do not become degenerate. In a similar way, ninjutsu has survived, uncorrupted and healthy, for close to a millennium, through a wide variety of circumstances. This is a fact. After all, everything that is not basically healthy—plant, person, enterprise, or idea—tends to fall by the wayside, to die, to disappear. And this is why I have resolved to maintain the health of this thousand-year-old tradition with all my heart and strength. The kind of thing that destroys the balance and endangers health is people's lusting after name and fame and fortune and power. But the spirit must be maintained strong, true, and uncorrupted.

Jack's successful 5th *dan* test. He has beautifully avoided the sword coming down from behind by rolling aside (*oten-taihenjutsus*). This is where the study of real *budo* begins. The fighting arts are not concerned with intellectual knowledge: they rightfully belong to the little-known world of the subconscious.

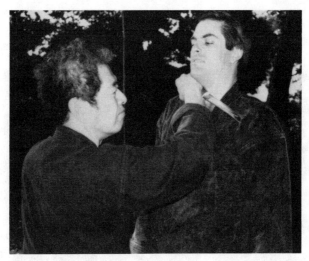

Jack Hoban with the author, practicing *shoto shirahadori*. As the attacker tries to cut, the chin is used momentarily to block the hand.

Jack is very quick at finding the weak points of a weapon and taking advantage of them. He's got guts!

Jack has just published a book on ninja *bojutsu* techniques, so let's see how he looks on the receiving end of such a lesson!

Holding the *hanbo* (short stick) in one hand like a walking stick, let's practice using it either for attacking or for defense and counterattack against an assailant (Jack) with a short sword.

First, the *hanbo* is swung with the right hand from the right side to attack the opponent's fingers holding the sword.

Then, the stick is swung up from below to hit the right wrist or hand. Lowering the posture makes this strike more effective.

Here, against a full-length sword, the defender springs up, striking the wrist either on the way up or as he lands.

After this strike, the stick is swung back into the left hand, and the end protruding beyond the gripping hand is used to rap Jack's wrist once more. As the stick is swung forward again with the right hand, yet another blow can be delivered to the wrist.

It is essential that mind and body work together in harmony if any high degree of skill is to be achieved. For this, a weapon has to become an extension of the ninja's body.

Following the above moves, the attacker's right hand can be trapped under the arm. Simultaneously, the right hand is slid up the *hanbo*, using it to attack the left side of the neck.

Next in sequence (not photographed), Jack's right hand could be broken (*kisai-gata*) as part of the natural flow of the defender's movement.

As these photos suggest, only if a person is accomplished in *taijutsu* can a weapon "come to life" in his hands and be used efficiently.

Kerikakaedori (trapping the kicking leg). The defender shifts his body to allow the kicking leg to fall into his hand, and then moves at will while lightly supporting or lifting it.

Tsukikeri (a kick in reply to a punch). Moving the body away from the punch, the defender uses the full length of the toes to kick just as the striking hand reaches its limit, and to bring the assailant down.

Ryoyokudori (catching both "wings"). Both arms are drawn back, and the opponent is controlled by bending or twisting the fingers of both hands.

Using *kerisedori* (catching the kicking leg behind the back), the defender applies pressure to the knee joint or a vital point with the right elbow.

Nageotoshi (throwing down). In the flow of this technique, the instant after the thrown opponent hits the floor, the kick puts him out of action.

Futaridori (controlling two opponents). In this technique, in response to the punching and kicking attacks of the assailants, the defender can make use of the force of their attacks to throw them and even subdue them.

Ittohdori (catching a sword) using a *shuko*.

Kakushisashi (hidden stab), also known as *mesashi* (eye stabbing).

Oh-ono tentai no jutsu: a flying attack using the great axe.

Bisentoh nagitaoshi no jutsu: mowing down opponents with a *naginata* (halberd).

Naginata haraigiri (sweeping cut with the halberd).

Shinobiyari gyakuzashi no jutsu (stabbing in the back with a "hidden" spear). The opponent's arms are taken back and he is finished off with the spear.

Performing the *kuji*. Without long training leading to the mastery of *taijutsu*, any attempt at performing the *kuji* is meaningless.

Taihenjutsu (defensive body movement) is used so as to allow a *moguriuchi* ("burrowing punch" using the thumb tip—also called *kage no ken*, or "shadow fist") to stop within a hair's breadth of a vital point.

Kakushigiri ("hidden cut"), a *kunoichi* (female ninja) technique. The flowers are flicked in the opponent's eyes to blind him with the pollen, and he is downed with the cut of a small knife hidden in the stems.

Kasagakure ("umbrella hiding"). After being suddenly opened in an attacker's face, an umbrella can be used for thrusting at the surprised man's eyes or other sensitive spots.

III

H: And now, just before we proceed to the next part of the interview, I'd like to say that Charles Daniel is the first of my American students to pass the fifth *dan* test the first time he took it. Of course, you, Doron, also passed it first time around. But in the old days, you *had* to pass it the first time you did it: it was a matter of survival then, because a real sword was used! If you didn't get it the first time in those days, it was clear that you didn't amount to much. But by the time you do your fifth *dan* test, the teacher knows pretty well if you're going to succeed. And anyone who makes a practice of staking a great deal on a single endeavor generally knows beforehand whether he is going to make a success of it or not.

It's true that there are times when you can't tell. But you've just got to "go for it," whatever you think. That's what we call in ninjutsu *"shiki wo shinobu."*[1]

---

1 Impossible to translate literally, this phrase indicates swallowing one's concerns and giving one's all, no matter what the consequences. It also contains the idea of putting one's trust in a higher, or deeper, consciousness.

Charles Daniel, 6th *dan*

Charles Daniel has experience in fighting arts from several countries, and is constantly working to understand the essential nature of *budo*.

After Charles passed his fifth *dan* test, I suggested that he should put his impressions in writing, to which he replied, "What is really of significance surely lies in what is *not* put into words."—a statement a little reminiscent of Miyamoto Musashi. He has the makings of a real martial artist.

With no thought for either winning or losing, you just go all out, regardless. It's utterly simple, but extremely difficult. Just as my teacher used to tell us, this kind of transcendence is really vital. In the fifth *dan* test, it is said that you go into a state of *mu*, nothingness, and this state is intrinsically a transcendental one. And I want you all to experience and appreciate this state, this sense of transcending.

However, it happens occasionally that you get involved in your own feelings and you feel you're unable to rise above them. At these times, there's no way to achieve the state of transcendence unless you can let go and get away from yourself. It's nothing complex or sophisticated—just very, very simple. That's what I have done—surrendered myself and dropped entirely the sense of being Grandmaster. I must distance myself from the ordinary actions, good or bad, of everyday life, in order to live an unattached, unconfined life. This is essential.

This is where those who become teachers all make a mistake, and the grander they want to be in other people's eyes, the bigger the error. Those who are after money are also off the track. Such people cause all sorts of difficulties, and this is the reason for the problems that have plagued ninjutsu in countries around the world. But perhaps now most aspects of the first "ninja boom" have disappeared from among my students. Instead, now, we have some genuine teachers, such as Doron, Charles, and Jack Hoban. At last, there are now people in other countries who are searching for and working toward the *real* ninjutsu, the *true budo*. And in Sweden, too, there are people, particularly Sven-Erik Bogsater,[2] who are also after the real thing. These people have really grown and made great progress.

And so I see this as a new period for ninjutsu, in which people who are interested in genuine ninjutsu are appearing. I am, of course, teaching ninjutsu, but I succeeded to the leadership of nine schools. But the grades that are awarded all over the world are grades only in ninpo *taijutsu*. I could also teach a whole lot of other things, like the *daken taijutsu* of the Shinden Fudoryu school, for example, or *jujutsu*, and so on, and I do want people all around the world to know that the *Bujinkan dojo* is not merely confined to

2 Passed fifth *dan* test, March 1987.

ninpo *taijutsu*. But ninpo *taijutsu* is nothing less than a great art: it's a magnificent thing ... and even if the *Bujinkan* were founded only on this one art, it would not be such a terrible pity or loss, in my opinion.

So I believe that now, as time passes, more and more people will appear who are interested in the pursuit of truth ... people like Doron, of course, and Charles, here. And when these two gentlemen return to their respective countries, or, for that matter, travel around the world, I want them to make the beauties of just this one art clear to people, wherever they are, not just by talking about them, but by demonstrating them in practice. Too often up till now, what has happened is that people unable to demonstrate the art have just been talking or writing about it and have been using it for their own self-glorification. There has been altogether too much claptrap. But now the claptrap is gradually going to be silenced, and the eyes of people all over the world will turn toward Japan and toward me.

Doron is a man who has always been after the truth about things. Now, we have Charles, who also passed the test the first time—becoming the first after Doron to do so. It's really very pleasing and encouraging, indeed.

So now, Charles, I wonder what you want to ask me. . . .

Charles Daniel (C): My first question is very general, and it has to do with your own lifestyle and your ideas for a proper lifestyle—why you live the way you do. And I'd like you, please, to point out some of the mistakes people make in their general lifestyles as they try to learn *budo*.

H: Well, I've mentioned that I spend a lot of my time taking walks, OK?—something like two hours a day, hmm? Eating whole rice and tofu, and so on, right? But I live quite immoderately. Most people maintain their health by living a life of moderation.

They live correctly, early to bed, early to rise, not eating too much, and so on, right? But there are others who live the way I live, too: I'm not the only one. People whose way of life is a constant in-the-moment practical training manage to carry on without the usual restraints and controls in their lives: it's a matter of getting into another kind of rhythm. So, as you know, on my trip to the U.S., I only slept a couple of hours a night for two weeks. Ten full days of that was spent actively teaching and demonstrating to the students there. I think that everyone there then began to understand what true ninjutsu is all about, and since that time, May of this year (1986), there have been a lot of people reexamining their ideas of the true nature of ninjutsu. And after that there came my election to the Hall of Fame as Instructor of the Year for 1986.

Fighting seems to be an integral part of life on Earth. If you take an overall look at human history, you see that, for every sixteen days of war, there has been only a single day or so of peace. One can't help thinking how much man must love war. If man stopped his warring, the earth would get overpopulated. But the human being is a destructive creature—even spoiling the earth itself; man destroys even the very place where he lives. What an idiotic animal, hmm? We ought to reflect upon such things very, very seriously. It's a bit like the lemmings—you know—how they commit mass suicide?

But it's quite possible to live even if one's life is irregular. I have many doubts about what is now thought of as a correct way of living in the modern world. What people regard as the right way to live nowadays reminds me of growing plants in greenhouse conditions: the results tend to be the opposite of hardy. People nowadays live in a kind of vegetative state—they're not really alive at all. The time will come when people will be needed who can live anywhere at all. When that happens, I will be happy with two hours of sleep a night. But it's important to create a different pattern and rhythm of living, and also to avoid fears of all kinds.

People are far too afraid of all sorts of things in their lives. They fear for their health; they have fears about how strong they are; they fear for their safety, and so on. On the other hand, when I go to Tokyo and people tell me how hair-raising it is to be driven by young Muramatsu here, it doesn't scare me at all! *(Laughter)* Seriously, though, it's essential to rid oneself of fear. Fear prevents people from doing so many things. They look after themselves far *too* well. If people would only not take so much care of themselves and have a little more confidence in themselves, a bit of courage—my teacher used to say that if one had no courage, there was no hope—with courage, anything can be accomplished. Also, faith and belief are essential.

Now, these are not things that are limited merely to religion, of course. There must be somebody with whom one has mutual faith: perhaps a parent, a lover, a child. Such a frame of mind is extremely important. In countries with a material civilization, such as the United States, it is considered necessary to have material things, and children are brought up with this idea. (That's not intended as a disparagement of the U.S.) But a material culture has its weak points. *Things* become important. Japan, too, is a nation with a materialistic culture, and the number of people here who are very weak has increased tremendously. So I believe that this is a period in which the balance between nature and material things is very carefully maintained, and people think about it a great deal. The really cultured man today gives importance to such a balance in his own life. And a truly cultured nation does the same, nations like America and Russia—China, too—where culture is highly advanced.

However, there are people who say that culture is a trivial thing. Indeed, "culture" alone doesn't mean much: there has to be a balance. With some people—especially the self-promoting ones—culture is a load of claptrap and grows out of their own complexes. They produce their kind of art out of their own hunger and desperation. It is a last resort, squeezed out from a position of weakness. The more they talk about it, the less they know, the less they are.

But those people who realize that they are ordinary are the truly cultured people. The true *budoka* remains ordinary at all times. His skills are not for show or for talk, but for use only at moments when there is a need for defense. And he works from balance, and therefore from strength.

C: The next question is also very general. In every person's life there are different stages, as he grows older. How do you regard the stages in the life of a martial artist, a martial arts life? I'm not talking just about rank, but about the general inner development of the person. And could you please give us some idea of the stages that people pass through while studying martial arts?

H: For me, it's mainly a matter of the person's destiny and of his love.

D: Destiny and love?

H: Yes. You see, why do I practice *budo*? Simply because I like *budo*, I love *budo*. So I'm stuck with it! When you love something you go through a stage when you become blind to the things around you—"Love is blind," right? If you can love someone who is complete and well-balanced, you can make a good home. A healthy, respectful kind of love will produce fine, healthy children. In the same way, I now have good *deshi* like Doron and Charles here. My love, my "children," seem to have appeared out of nothingness, out of nowhere. If that weren't so, my wife would give me hell! *(Laughter)* But I think one should consider how miraculous it is that our children always appear

out of nothing. Everybody says that they are the
products of the parents, but I believe that they appear out of a void.

There are so many blessings that come out of that
emptiness. . . . It reminds me of the painter Okamoto
Taro, who says that his creations appear like explo-
sions out of nowhere. And you know what they used to
say about the wise old hermits, that they ate the mists
of the mountains, that they lived on space alone? Well,
"eating mist, living on space" doesn't refer to swallowing stuff down one's throat: it's about *feeling* the
space, with your skin. You see, we have to interpret
the word "eat" here to mean taking another kind of
"food" into oneself, not physical, but mental or spiritual food.

I've never discussed this before, but "eating," when
it referred to those hermits, didn't mean what we
usually think. They were people who were able to
stay alive through the sensitivity of their entire bod-
ies. The soul has its own food that gives it nourish-
ment, and the mind has its food, just as the body does.
Books can be food; a meeting with a good person can
also nourish one—and the finer and more beautiful
that person's character, the more uplifting it can be.
And when you are satisfied, you can share your food,
just as, once you have realized something, you can
share that realization. You also learn to discriminate
and to recognize that the ideas one person has to offer
are an unhealthy form of food. You begin gradually,
through training, to accept only things that are naturally good. This is really very important. And animals in the wild, of course, won't generally eat food
that would be harmful to them. It's only man that
eats virtually anything at any level, healthy or unhealthy! That's why man has to undergo training and
why he has been blessed with people to guide him,
with intelligence, and so on.

Since man was created in such a way that he is

deprived of these instinctive things, the Creator has provided him instead with the ability to accumulate knowledge. But together with the knowledge, he also possesses foolishness. It's rather like the oxygenated, "red" blood of the arteries in contrast with the depleted, "blue" blood of the veins. But I didn't pick up these ideas by studying them: I am speaking directly from my own experience. And in one way, one might liken intellectual things to physical objects, whereas those in the subconscious are not at all physical and are considerably more important, and it's necessary to begin thinking in this direction.

But it is really a very significant thing that we three—Doron, Charles, and myself—have got together to discuss these things, these deeper questions which are not generally associated with the martial arts. It is my duty as Grandmaster to bring out those aspects that are important—like the other day, when I had photos of ninjutsu in action taken (for publication) in such a way that the faces and their expressions were cut out. There were objections to this, but martial arts publications are full of unnecessary and exaggerated facial expressions, which are just so much show: just bogus and false. Those who believe themselves to be outstanding are really very prosaic. It is only the ordinary man who is truly extraordinary!—And satori is only a step away. . . . I am talking about the essence of *budo*. And the essence is really very simple.

You know, Takamatsu Sensei only used to talk about the most important things. He would never answer questions clearly for a student who was not yet prepared, because of the confusion it might cause later. Years after, sometimes, we realized that this was the right way for us: that we had to learn for ourselves. He used to teach very quickly. There was no time to think; it was just one technique after another. That's how I was able to pick up the essence efficiently, and that's how I teach now. What I want you to do is just take it as it is. *Don't* think too much. If you get involved with thinking about it, the whole thing gets lost or loses its purity. Don't think during practice—*do!* The more you think, the further from the truth of *budo* you get: *budo* is *not* an academic subject!

Anyway, to get back to the question. . . . First, it's necessary to speak about the stages of training under Takamatsu Sensei and those with me. I think this is the best way of talking about the stages involved.

Over the period of his childhood, Takamatsu Sensei was brought up by nine different women who played the role of mother, and not only were there financial difficulties and a scarcity of food, but also he was a rather sickly child. As a result, I am told, when he was small he was pretty much of a weakling, but he was given training under three teachers: his uncle, Toda Shinryuken Sensei, and then Ishitani Sensei and Mizuta Sensei. Later, in Korea, on his way to China when he was about fifteen, he became a student of a teacher called Kim Kei-Mei. But first, as I say, he was this unfortunate weakling and was put in the charge of his uncle, Toda Sensei, and practiced *budo* under him. He really didn't want to at first, but soon he came to love *budo*, and he kept that love for the rest of his life. His teacher used to train him to the point of exhaustion. When he was still a boy, he used to carry, over his shoulders, buckets full of water up to the top of the hill where his father's factory was— but not just the usual two: he used to carry *four* at a time! He used to do this regularly, so that his legs and hips became very strong.

But later, you know, he secluded himself in the mountains. This was not for the sake of his *budo* training: it happened like this. . . . In his early twenties, after he came back from his first stay in China, he lived in his grandmother's house. At this time, he was suffering from beriberi and some kind of lung disease. He'd already been told that his condition was incurable, but he thought he would go to his grandmother's house—she was one of the women who had brought him up, you see—to try to recuperate. He didn't want to be a burden to her, though, and he decided to leave.

So, taking a few pounds of whole rice with him, he went off into the mountains to be alone, perhaps to die there, and stayed by the Kame-no-o Falls. There, in the midst of nature, by living on natural food—fruits and nuts from the trees, and so on—and on the fresh air of the mountains, he managed to recover his health. There was also an ascetic mountain monk there, known as Old Man Tamaoki, who found him lying there. (Just after Takamatsu Sensei arrived at that spot, he spent most of his time on his back and could get around only by crawling. He would wash his rice in the river and just leave it on a rock in the sun to split open, and he would then eat it.) One day, Old Man Tamaoki came and found him there and told him that he had tapeworms. "We'll have to get rid of them," he said, and started to chant an incantation.

Well, Takamatsu Sensei had his own ideas about such things and apparently said, "Come on, old man, you don't expect *that* to work, do you?" By that time, he didn't care whether he died or not. But a week later, a huge tapeworm—almost the size of two bowls of noodles—came out of him. Soon, he was full of life again. He began practicing his *budo* again, using the trees and rocks around him in whatever way he could for his training. As a result of his training, he had become highly sensitive to many things; for example, as I have mentioned, he was able to tell intuitively the sex and age of anyone approaching, before they came within range of sight or hearing. After about a year of living like this, he had grown a long, shaggy beard and finally came down from the mountains. He then became a Buddhist priest, and so on; but it seems that by this time his extraordinary psychic powers were already well developed. Something like this happened to me, too.

But the reason why I took up *budo* was that my father was an alcoholic, and I needed to protect myself. I started practicing a whole range of martial arts—judo, karate, kendo, all that I could find. I did a tremendous amount of training, and even things like sword-catching became a part of me. Then, one day, in connection with all this study and practice, I met Takamatsu Sensei and started following him. I knew that he was the real thing. I feel so lucky in having found him, because many, many people fail to make that connection with something real.

Some of the people who have come to me, too, fail to see how real and genuine what I am teaching is, and they leave. The student alienates himself from the teacher: someone thinks he is learning, or pretends he understands, but really doesn't learn much or understand at all—there are many people like this. And they're really in a sad situation, I think. It's a result of their own desires and ambitions. Their own "Streetcar Named Desire" becomes derailed! But the teaching itself is not such a difficult thing to comprehend—as long as you love it. It's like the proverb of the devoted wife who is willing to live anywhere, do anything, for her beloved. Someone, something you can love for an entire lifetime: that is what's real. You must be able to trust it; the respect and the appreciation must be there. . . . The respect and the gratitude must never be forgotten. But if you start giving your respect to something that is contrived, false, not genuine, then you're really in trouble. That's what real training is all about. It's not some complex concept.

My search is always directed toward finding the truth; and one thing that that involves is a certain amount of sacrifice—"Nothing ventured, nothing gained"—but a person has to be wholehearted in order to gain something true. It's like the old Japanese martial art epigram,[3] which goes,

Hell gapes beneath the upraised sword. . . .
Step *in*! And Heaven is your reward!

When the moment of truth comes, we each have a single choice: to step ahead or to run away. For me, it must constantly be the former alternative. And it's like the *Sennichi Kaihogyo*[4] practice of the Buddhist priests, in which they practice careful walking day after day as a method of achieving *satori*, enlightenment. At the same time, of course, the "walking," the searching, the learning, proceeds internally, in the heart, and can continue even if the use of the legs is lost. This is one reason why I walk every day, too. And in fact, you know, the word "walking" implies right conduct in all aspects of one's life.

C: Could you please tell us a few of the highlights in your own training, from the time you first began till today? For example, from the time when you were training with Takamatsu Sensei?

H: The real highlight of that time was when I became seriously ill! For five years just after my teacher made me *Iemoto*, I got only about three hours of sleep a day, because of the great amount of work that fell to me in activities for the mass media. I was also doing my daily work and my ninpo study and training. As I said before, I received the title of *Iemoto* somewhat ahead of time, and it was not until September 21 last year, fifteen years after Takamatsu Sensei passed away, and 30 years after he

---

3 Hundreds of such epigrams existed as short, simple poems of no set form containing distillations of the teachings and truths (the "secrets") of the martial arts for ready transmission to students and disciples. This one reads in Japanese: *"Furiageshi tachi no shita koso jigoku nari, tada fumikomeya saki wa gokuraku."*
4 Literally, "Thousand-day Liberation Training."

gave me the title, that I finally realized I was a real *Iemoto*. This is nothing strange: I simply didn't at the time have the capability. But, as a man, I had to fulfill the responsibilities of my position. However, that time became an outstanding time for me because of the continuous five-year period with so little sleep, which led to an autonomic nervous imbalance so that I could hardly see, my intestines were in a terrible state, I was unable even to stand properly, and so on. But I still loved the training. Even though I was sometimes unable to avoid being thrown and hit in practice by my own students, I still never stopped training.

And during that time, one of the closest friends I had betrayed me by breaking a promise to me. But, as it turned out, it was a very good lesson for me. I learned the need for independence, and it gave me a lot of inner strength.

I did not feel hate for him, and in fact realized—it was like a *satori* for me—the value of his action was an opportunity for my growth. It was like a gift from the gods for me. The ninja must live, after all, without self-pity, without regret. Through this learning process, my health returned. I had to carry out my responsibilities. My body then became lighter, and many other changes took place. But it's necessary not to take a betrayal like that badly, even if it's perpetrated by an intimate friend. It's really like the fifth *dan* test: you know, in Japanese, the word for *betray* is "to cut down from behind," and even to be betrayed by a *deshi* should not be judged as a bad thing, any more than being attacked from behind in the fifth *dan* test should be judged as "bad." "Good" and "bad" are, after all, only parts of the same continuum, but it is up to us to choose the good through our attitude and through our perception. The betrayal doesn't matter to me. I was able to overcome it, and that too became a highlight of my training. It is no obstacle for me.

People create all their barriers for themselves. It's really such a foolish thing to do. We create our own obstacles and lose our own way in the search for truth. So it represents no barrier for me now. All that it's necessary to do when one faces a barrier is just keep walking, paying it no attention. Just keep going, keep walking, and the obstacles disappear! In my case, when I seem to be in trouble and I think I won't make it, I just keep walking. And so it continues, even today. Those sorts of things were the real highlights for me.

But even when you are on the receiving end of some painful attack, you can feel the pain well enough— and even that can have some element of enjoyment in it since it's part of practice, without there being any masochism or sadism involved. Even a technique that makes you cry out in pain, you see it, but you don't get how it's done. It becomes like an interesting puzzle, and you feel so happy when you solve it! And then, when you teach it to your students, you see them puzzling over the same problems as you yourself did—it's really very amusing! And those are some more highlights! And this kind of attitude to things is also very important.

C: What is the meaning of the title *"Soke"* (Grandmaster), and some of the differences between a *Soke* and somebody who's just a very good technician?

H: *"Soke"* signifies nothingness, zero, emptiness, void. Something that exists, and yet does not. The *Soke* is just an ordinary person, and yet, somehow, he is someone who is living his life according to some invisible divine command. You see, I do not live by my conscious mind, not at all, so that whatever I have thought up till now can just suddenly change in my mind, though it is not a consciously engineered change. The *Bujinkan* has changed, too, right? And because it can change, it can improve—as I think it does with every change—right? All sorts of things have happened over the years, and all of these have been lessons for all of us, including myself. That's why progress continues constantly.

In Japanese, we speak of the *seirobyoshi*, the four inevitable phases of living—birth, aging, illness, and death. And, like life itself, a person's training inevitably involves "bad" things as well as "good." And that's just as it should be. Otherwise, one could not save a person, one could not protect a person. Not that we in martial arts are involved in "saving" people: that's the job of the religious people. *Budoka* protect and defend people. But still, we don't protect people who don't deserve protection—troublemakers, criminals, and the like. The mission of the *Bujinkan* is to protect the good.

C: This question is more for the American martial arts community, where the most confusion is. There have been a tremendous number of books and articles written on how ninjutsu is connected with certain religions and things of that nature. Could you speak about the role of religions such as Zen, *Shugendo*,[5] or *Mikkyo* in the practice of ninpo, and maybe clarify that once and for all?

H: Yes, there is a relationship, and there are influences. But, to be frank, among the people involved in religion, there are some pretty rotten characters. There's no way that you could say that all those who associate themselves with religions are outstanding people worthy of our deep respect. This has to be acknowledged first of all. So *Mikkyo*, for example, may be a wonderful religion, and some of its scriptures may be magnificent, but it's really important to keep one's eyes wide open to observe the true character of someone who gets himself caught up with religion. We all know of so-called religious people, priests as well as others, who are after the money they can

---

5 The way of the ascetic mountain monk in Japan.

get out of it, who spend their evenings in Ginza bars. So *Mikkyo* and Zen . . . and even in Zen, to which outstanding men of religion like Sogen Omori belong, there are those who charge money for a rank in the temple hierarchy. But I'm not saying that money itself is necessarily bad, of course.

I happen to think that the more mysterious side of Zen, the intangible aspects of it, are really wonderful. But you don't need to worry much about these religions; and I myself don't feel that Zen or *Mikkyo*, for example, deserve much attention. You can easily see their bad points. After all, it is one characteristic of the *budoka* to home in immediately on the weaknesses, the openings.

I was invited to make a speech before some Buddhist priests at Mount Hiei the other day. One thing that I told them was that I could understand the feelings of Oda Nobunaga.[6] Now, I believe that there is corruption in religion all over the world. Nobody should consider that Zen and *Mikkyo* are beyond reproach. A man should look at the world with his own eyes. No one can see or judge clearly if he bows his head down and believes what somebody else says right from the start. To make an analogy, I think that the psychology of the Western custom of shaking hands is excellent—looking into each other's eyes and linking hands. The Japanese bow and lower their eyes, especially when the person being greeted has seniority or authority, so that their vision is limited. This is true where religion is concerned, also, both literally and metaphorically, or psychologically.

On the other hand, as I wrote in a book some time ago, it is possible to "see," even without using the eyes, and to "hear," even without the ears—which is

---

6 A great feudal warlord who broke the military and political power that had been amassed by the temples on Mount Hiei in the late sixteenth century.

why the Buddhist statue that I made of Takamatsu
Sensei has neither eyes nor ears. This featurelessness
also represents the "nothingness" of the true Grandmaster. The whole statue is covered with a golden
color. In ninpo, you see, your *whole body* must act as
your eyes and ears. This was one thing that helped
me realize that I had at last become a proper
Grandmaster.

Some of the things that have been happening in the
United States are quite ridiculous. There is all this
weird stuff like religious ninpo; and then, people who
have no experience of ninjutsu are writing about it.
Of course, they are way off track. This kind of thing
is really disturbing—it's all quite wrong. So, one
point I'd like to emphasize is that, in any venture, the
nature of the human being must never be forgotten—
and there's nothing mysterious about that!

C: One more question for the public: in many of the
older martial arts schools in Japan, the idea seems to
be just to preserve what they've got, not to change
anything in their practice. The idea with the Bujinkan is apparently a little bit different. Would you
give us your thoughts on how you see the martial arts
evolving, changing, or adapting to the times?

H: What has to be remembered about such preser-
vation is that what is kept is just the form, not the
essence. It's just an aspect of materialistic culture, a
type of materialism. And there's a tendency for *budo*
like these to survive. There are, it's true, some spiritually fine and good teachers in them, but for *budo* it
is not enough just to have a good heart and some
spiritual understanding, because the truth of *budo*
always encompasses two opposing aspects: *yin* and
yang, good and bad, weak and strong, win and loss, as
well as the deceptive and the obvious or the false and
the true that are both components of a shrewd tactic
or a tricky technique.[7] This is where the problem lies
with *budo*. Of course, even within form, it is essential

that this duality should be comprehended, since the forms are set in motion by people, and the people are set in motion by their minds. I'd better not say any more than this, but try to grasp the feeling of what I'm getting at.

Once, Takamatsu Sensei said to me, "Hatsumi, nobody's gone as far as you have." I'm not saying this out of conceit or anything. But when I look back at so many things, I see that he was always quietly helping us, always teaching us in his quiet way. He never sought any kind of publicity. It was almost as if he were devoting his life to passing on what he knew to just one person. I am so deeply grateful to him for what he gave me. For me, too, just one person would be enough. Although I have many students, just one who would understand would be enough, just one who would understand—not my ideas so much as the essential flow of all *budo*. And that is why I am teaching.

C: Finally, another quick question for the public: could you say something about the many rival ninjutsu organizations that exist in America and Europe, and how you feel about that sort of thing?

H: It's just childish. They're just playing at ninjutsu, like children having childish fights and rivalries. So a bit of trouble here and there can't be helped. Doron and Charles, you're beyond that (like their "big brothers"!), so I know you understand this. To be frank, the whole thing's silly and trivial. What they're doing has nothing to do with what I teach. They're wasting all their efforts on things I haven't taught. If they'd practice proper ninjutsu, it would be OK, but they don't know what it is. But that's all

---

7 After "because," Dr. Hatsumi's words here were merely, "in *budo* there is *kyojitsu*." The word *kyojitsu* (literally, "false-true") implies all the other ideas mentioned, and more: from a simple ruse, through tact and diplomacy, to the duality and relativity of life, and even truth itself.

right, now that people like you, who understand
clearly what my ninjutsu is all about, will be going
around teaching. And if you'll pass on what I've given
you, those things will just fizzle out.

Ninjutsu in the West will begin to grow up now. So
far, we've had the "Ninja Children's Group"!
(Chuckles) Now, with the emergence of people like
Doron and Charles, we're going to move on to the
"Boys, be ambitious!" stage, and ninpo in the West
will enter its adolescence. And that's just as it should
be: the childish stage is passing, and certainly there's
no reason for me to get upset about it.

In essence, the European martial arts are the same as the
Oriental.

Katate-nuki no kamae—one-
handed sword-drawing
posture.

The ninja can use a sword to dazzle and disconcert an attacker who is about to draw his sword, or is advancing to attack. It was important in more senses than one for the ninja to be in the shadow of his sword—perhaps one of the reasons for his nickname *kage*, or shadow. Use of both the dark and the light-reflecting aspects of his weapons is part of the ninja's arts of deception and surprise.

As Charles Daniel tries to draw his sword, he is first momentarily blinded, as in the previous photo, and is then controlled or subdued by the adversary's sword. If he moves, he gets cut—a concept important in many senses in ninjutsu. All of this is part of the ninja's practice, as he "speaks with both body and mind."

Happo no kamae (eight-direction stance). This is not a fixed stance since its direction shifts.

Jumoji no kamae (cross stance). The cross (+) in a circle is used as a symbol of the eradication of evil.

Keribarai no kamae (kick-sweeping stance).

Juji shinobigatana no kamae (hidden-sword cross stance). A stance used with ninja weapons.

Shuto uchi (striking with the hand-blade). The strike is made with body and hand acting in concert, the power coming from the body movement.

Kerinuki (kicking through).
For attacking vital points.

Nageuchi no kamae (flinging-strike stance).

Nageuchi no kamae. Striking as if the fist is being thrown at its target.

Hicho no kamae
(flying bird stance).

Hicho tai ate no kamae
(flying bird body-striking stance).

All movements flow from one posture to another.

For thrown weapons, the mind must act as a kind of radar. Even if the target moves, as long as this "mental radar" is operating properly, the target's motion is followed perfectly.

Senban uchi: holding the *shuriken* (throwing star).

Senban nage no kamae (*Shuriken*-throwing posture).

Boshuriken (dart)-throwing stance.

The completed posture of
the dart throw.

Secrets of the *kukinage* ("air" throw). The keys to this
technique are the use of the opponent's own force, and a
grasp of psychological factors. The thrower does not even
touch the partner's body, but directs his mind so as to throw
him.

Hand-held wooden cannons, strengthened by wrapping and gluing on many layers of paper. Both large and medium-sized weapons can be seen.

The hand-held cannon would contain rusty iron fragments so as to act like a shotgun and cause maximum casualties when a ninja was outnumbered.

A technique of concealment: the *taijutsu* of moving about in the mist, known as *muton yuho*.

The author with Andy Adams, an American who wrote a book about ninjutsu. Some 30 years ago, Donn Draeger also came to research material for "This Is Japan." Introducing ninjutsu to the world, when even the Japanese knew so little of it, must have been quite a task!

A team from West Germany's national television network came to film ninjutsu. At last, the truth about ninjutsu, what I have been trying to teach for so long, is beginning to reach the world. . . .